D0443491

Praise for *THE END OF ABSENCE*

"Michael Harris has written an important book for our information-overloaded times of ironic hashtag conversations and idealized online avatars. *The End of Absence* is a forceful, insightful, and ultimately human reminder to us all that information is not wisdom, that speed is not depth, that in the pauses of solitude come authenticity and surprise, and that the empty spaces we so desperately and busily have sought to fill in, as he writes, never were so barren after all."

—Brigid Schulte, author of the *New York Times* bestselling *Overwhelmed*

"*The End of Absence* is an extraordinary chronicle for an extraordinary time, a moment when humanity went from dropping out to turning on 24/7. Michael Harris is here to remind future generations of what it's like to miss nothing—literally nothing—and in so doing, he examines what we've lost and what we've gained (and what hasn't changed). This is the rare kind of book that will change the way you see the world."   —Arjun Basu, author of *Waiting for the Man*

"*The End of Absence* offers a deeply compelling perspective that forces us to acknowledge an uncomfortable truth: ours is the last generation that will have known a pre-digital world. Michael Harris's provocative book tells us why that matters and encourages us to be more thoughtful as we prepare for the future."

—Amy Webb, author of *Data, A Love Story*

"Digging its heels firmly into the slippery slope of the digital avalanche threatening to bury us, *The End of Absence* is a passionate, astute, honest, sympathetic account of how to stay sane in a manic culture. Thoreau would have been delighted to add this knowing, poetic book to his small shelf in the Walden cabin. A superb guide to our present disaster, as well as a meditation on where we might be if we could relearn our ability to pause, even for a moment."

—Tim Blackmore, author of *War X*

"We are at a singular moment where information, once scarce, is suddenly ubiquitous. Michael Harris asks what this moment means, and answers with insight, humor, and great humanity. A must-read for anyone curious about how the digital revolution is changing our culture and ourselves." —Nora Young, author of *The Virtual Self*

THE END OF ABSENCE

Reclaiming What We've Lost in a World of Constant Connection

Michael Harris

Current

CURRENT
Published by the Penguin Group
Penguin Group (USA) LLC
375 Hudson Street
New York, New York 10014

USA I Canada I UK I Ireland I Australia I New Zealand I India I South Africa I China
penguin.com
A Penguin Random House Company

First published by Current, a member of Penguin Group (USA) LLC, 2014

A portion of this book first appeared as "Hot Wired" in *The Walrus.*

LIBRARY OF CONGRESS CATALOGING-IN-PUBLICATION DATA
Harris, Michael, date.
   The end of absence : reclaiming what we've lost in a world of constant connection /
Michael Harris.
      pages   cm
   Includes bibliographical references and index.
   ISBN 978-1-59184-693-2
1. Information society.   2. Information technology—Social aspects.
3. Internet—Social aspects.   4. Technology—Social aspects.
I. Title.

HM851.H3673   2014
302.23'1—dc23   2014009772

Printed in the United States of America
10 9 8 7 6 5 4 3 2 1

Set in Sabon
Designed by Spring Hoteling

FOR KENNY

CONTENTS

THE END OF ABSENCE

PROLOGUE
This Can Show You Everything

1996—Malaysia

THE settlement called Batu Lima sat deep in the tropical forests of eastern Malaysia, about three miles from the closest real village. Its one-room houses, largely abandoned or dismantled by the time our story begins, stood on stilts, with floors of bamboo. One family was left—made up of Siandim Gunda, Jimi Sinting, and their twelve children. One daughter, Linda Jimi, was fourteen years old and ready to leave.

There was a box with four little legs in their house, and in the box was a black-and-white television. There was no electricity (Linda was tasked with gathering firewood for the kitchen stove each day), but on special occasions, Linda's father would take the car battery that powered the TV into the village and have it charged. Then Linda could watch *Sesame Street,* which was senseless but wonderful, with its American children and Muppets prattling in confounding English, playing out their deeply foreign antics.

Big Bird was yellow, Linda learned. The village children had electricity and color televisions; they would brag about their colors.

Linda said, "I know," and told the other children that her family had colors, too.

Sesame Street was baffling, but Linda's family believed intrinsically in spirits and ghosts, so the apparitions that flashed on the television screen could be folded into a larger trust in magic, in brushes with the unknowable.

Besides, more magical by far was the *komburongoh* that Linda's grandmother Sukat wielded. Linda never touched the sacred object herself, for fear of angering the spirits and growing sick—but she could look across the hut at the thing in her grandmother's hands, a tight bundle of teeth taken from several animals, knotted together with a collection of small bones. Sukat, who could handle the *komburongoh* with impunity, had access to the spirit of an ancestor, and she could call upon the spirit for help when attempting to heal members of the Dusun tribe.

Once, before the village was abandoned, Linda watched her grandmother work her magic over a child who'd been stricken with fever. This was only a small ritual, so Sukat hadn't bothered to dress in the full garb of a *bobolian* (high priestess)—she'd worn an ordinary sarong and a long-sleeved blouse. Sukat had moved her *komburongoh* over the sickly child's head, shaking her bundle of teeth for five full minutes while the infant sweated beneath. Sukat had told the spirit to undo this child's illness, and the spirit had asked for a sacrifice—a chicken or a few cups of rice.

Sukat's healing powers were meant to be passed on to her daughter—Linda's mother—but Sukat died too early, and then, like many Malaysians, Linda's mother converted to Catholicism. When the family finally left Batu Lima and moved to town, Linda's mother left behind Sukat's mystical equipment.

Linda, too, was taking steps away from that miniature settlement, away from the mythical past of Malaysia. She wanted something more, though she couldn't say what "more" might look like. At eighteen, she ran away from home and moved to the city of Sabah (a relative metropolis with its two thousand people). There she worked at a KFC restaurant (much the same setup as the American version, though minus the American pay). She saved her meager wages for months before purchasing a mobile phone, which became precious to her. She wanted badly to enter the modern world, to live, at last, in the full glow of the world's future. Eventually, Linda worked her way up to the far "classier" Little Italy restaurant in Kota Kinabalu. The pay was the same, but at least tourists dined there, which meant Linda could practice her English.

Tourists like Nate, a Canadian who'd just graduated from college and was backpacking around the region. "Come hang out in Singapore with me," he offered.

"Sure," said Linda, and she went a little farther afield. The couple had their affair and Nate left for home, promising to return in the fall. Linda hoped, rather than believed, that the promise would be fulfilled. And when Nate did return, eventually inviting Linda to come live on the other side of the world, in Vancouver, she might well have undergone severe culture shock. The Canadian city was almost a letdown, though, since Linda had assumed that every city in North America looked like the city she'd seen, in black and white, on *Sesame Street*.

· · · · ·

A few years and many miles later, Linda returned to Malaysia. Now she was a soon-to-be Canadian, lugging a laptop to her mother's home. She patched into the Internet through a shaky dial-up connection and managed to introduce her mother to the wonder that is Google.

"This can show you everything," she told her mother. Videos of celebrities flashed across the laptop's screen. "Here, I'll show you where I live in Canada." A few taps later, the laptop's screen was displaying a map of the world and Linda proceeded to zoom into Canada, into British Columbia, into Vancouver, into the city's east side, and finally into the block where she lived with Nate. "There," she said to her mother, pointing. "That's where I live. That's my home." Her mother didn't understand at first, and Linda continued to wave at the screen. "This can show you everything."

"It can show me everything?" her mother asked, now leaning in, full of wonder.

"Everything. What do you want to see?"

The answer came through tears: "Show me my mother in the afterlife."

PART I

Gathering

We think we have discovered a grotto that is stored with bewildering treasure; we come back to the light of day, and the gems we have brought are false—mere pieces of glass—and yet does the treasure shine on, unceasingly, in the darkness.

—Maurice Maeterlinck

CHAPTER 1
This Kills That

Technology is neither good nor bad, nor is it neutral.

—Melvin Kranzberg

SOON enough, nobody will remember life before the Internet. What does this unavoidable fact mean?

For those billions who come next, of course, it won't mean anything very obvious. Our online technologies, taken as a whole, will have become a kind of foundational myth—a story people are barely conscious of, something natural and, therefore, unnoticed. Just as previous generations were charmed by televisions until their sets were left always on, murmuring as consolingly as the radios before them, future generations will be so immersed in the Internet that questions about its basic purpose or meaning will have faded from notice. Something tremendous will be missing from their lives—a mind-set that their ancestors took entirely for granted—but they will hardly be able to notice its disappearance. Nor can we blame them.

However, we have in this brief historical moment, this moment in between two modes of being, a very rare opportunity. For those of us who have lived both with and without the vast, crowded connectivity the Internet provides, these are the few days when we can still notice the difference between Before and After.

This is the moment. Our awareness of this singular position pops up every now and again. We catch ourselves idly reaching for our phones at the bus stop. Or we notice how, midconversation, a fumbling friend dives into the perfect recall of Google. We can still catch ourselves. We say, *Wait. . . .*

I think that within the mess of changes we're experiencing, there's a single difference that we feel most keenly; and it's also the difference that future generations will find hardest to grasp. That is the end of absence—the loss of lack. The daydreaming silences in our lives are filled; the burning solitudes are extinguished.

Before all memory of those absences is shuttered, though, there is this brief time when we might record what came before. We might do something with those small, barely noticeable instances when we're reminded of our love for absence. They flash at us amid the rush of our experience and seem to signal: *Wait, wasn't there something . . . ?*

I was shaken by one of these moments, one not-so-special day, at the offices of *Vancouver* magazine. I was employed there for years as an editor and staff writer. I was, to use the stultifying phrase we were offered, a "content creator."

. . . . .

I presume I'm late for work as I trundle over the Granville Street Bridge on the #10 bus toward the magazine offices. Out the window, I can monitor the gunmetal sky while licking at my knuckles where Starbucks dribbles down my hand. I wonder whether I'm (a) ten minutes late, which is acceptable, even advised; or (b) twenty minutes late, at which point one invites passive-aggressive comments.

Alas. It is (b). A jockish intern smiles—"So, you decided to join us"—as I move by his gray cubicle toward my own. I give a quick laugh to avoid seeming rude, but I don't slow my pace. Stopping leaves one open to requests for "coffee," which means career advice. These talks only depress me, since the interns tote such fierce and poorly researched ambitions. They stream from journalism schools, expecting internships to lead to jobs at magazines and newspapers, never quite believing the truth of our haggard faces.

Our business is ailing. Each magazine, like a freighter, groans in its effort to turn, to adapt to online life—but too slow, too slow. Some publications shutter; others collapse their international bureaus; all grow anorexic; sales departments, empowered by the desperation of publishers, are able to blur the lines between advertisements and editorial further and further. (When I brought up the old concept of church and state with a senior sales associate at one magazine, she chirped, "Oh, we *are* church and state. But, you know, *ish*.")

We aren't quite willing to see the writing on the wall. I took an editing job at *Vancouver* magazine in 2008, immediately before the global recession added dynamite to our industry's collapse. Corporate overlords in Montreal slashed a third of the jobs in the office. Meanwhile, the advent of digital technologies brought new responsibilities that we remaining few grudgingly took on each year. Ten years ago, no magazine editor imagined spending half the day maintaining Twitter feeds or refereeing comment trails on Facebook. But there we were, managing content instead of creating it. We spent most of our lives pushing electronic nothings around while staring at a glowing rectangle.

After an editorial meeting (where we're informed that our Twitter avatar lacks "punch"), I retreat to my cubicle and begin opening windows within windows on the two monitors that are always lit atop my desk. I begin to work on a small item about the Cirque du Soleil but am derailed seventy-five words in by a video of Anderson Cooper coming out of the closet that the art director has sent me via iChat. Another iChat window opens while I'm watching the video, this time a question from the editor in chief, which requires that I open my in-box to dig up an old e-mail. My mother, meanwhile, has e-mailed me on a separate account, asking me to bring that salad she likes to dinner tomorrow night. And so on. Within ten minutes I am partway through a dozen digital interactions, but none are complete. The jockish intern drifts by with a question of his own and I give him a clipped response, because at that moment he's just another window that I want to shut. Back in 1998, the writer Linda Stone coined the phrase that describes the state I'm in: "continuous partial attention." It's an impoverished state, but one I seem to welcome into my life every day.

Most of us at the magazine would actually become distraught if forced to complete a task before a new one was presented. I never ignore my computer's alerts; every ping from my phone is seen to. Dr. Gary Small, a researcher at UCLA, writes that "once people get used to this state, they tend to thrive on the perpetual connectivity. It feeds their egos and sense of self-worth, and it becomes irresistible." And I do, I suppose, feel a certain importance with all these pings, all these requests for connection hailing down on me. I must be very, very important. I must be needed, necessary, crucial. But something has changed since my initial few years at the magazine, something in my attitude toward the pings. What has changed?

Dr. Small points out that this atmosphere of manic disruption makes my adrenal gland pump up production of cortisol and adrenaline.

In the short run, these stress hormones boost energy levels and augment memory, but over time they actually impair cognition, lead to depression, and alter the neural circuitry in the hippocampus, amygdala, and prefrontal cortex—the brain regions that control mood and thought. Chronic and prolonged techno-brain burnout can even reshape the underlying brain structure.

Techno-brain burnout. That sounds about it. At one point that harried afternoon, I stop and count the number of windows open on my two monitors. Fourteen. As I count them up, my phone pings again and I look down at the text message glowing there:

```
Dude, are you alive or what?
```

The text is just a flick from an impatient friend, but in my distracted state I read it as a sincere question. *Are you alive or what?*

And that was the moment. I picked up the phone and, ignoring the message, switched on its camera function. I photographed my monitors, plastered over with e-mails and instant messages and Word files and .pdfs. Never forget that you don't *want* this, I thought. Never forget that you live in an ecosystem designed to disrupt you and it will take you for a ride if you let it.

Just before the magazine forfeited half its office space—a bid to consolidate ranks and bring in some money by subletting—I quit my job.

This left me with a distressing amount of free time—time I filled, initially, by reading about a moment weirdly similar to our own: the year 1450, when a German patrician called Johannes Gutenberg, after decades of tinkering and some very sketchy loans, managed to invent a printing press with movable type.

Like the Internet, Gutenberg's machine made certain jobs either ridiculous or redundant (so long, scriptoria). But much more was dismantled by Gutenberg's invention than the employment of a few recalcitrant scribes. As the fidelity and speed of copying was ratcheted way up, there was a boom in what we'd now call data transfer: A great sermon delivered in Paris might be perfectly replicated in Lyon. (Branding improved, too: for the first time subjects knew what their king looked like.) Such uniformity laid the groundwork for massive leaps in knowledge and scientific understanding as a scholastic world that was initially scattered began to cohere into a consistent international conversation, one where academics and authorities could build on one another's work rather than repeat it.[1] As its influence unfurled across Europe, the press would flatten entire monopolies of knowledge, even enabling Martin Luther to shake the foundations of the Catholic Church; next it jump-started the Enlightenment. And the printing press had its victims; its cheap and plentiful product undid whole swaths of life, from the recitation of epic poetry[2] to the authority of those few who could afford handmade manuscripts. In Blake Morrison's novel *The Justification of Johann Gutenberg,* he has the inventor arguing with an abbot not about the content his printing press creates, but about the *way* text can now be read. The abbot exclaims: "The word of God needs to be interpreted by priests, not spread about like dung."[3] The very fecundity of the press, its ability to free up content and make it cheaply available to the masses, made it a danger to the established powerhouse of the Catholic Church and a serious destabilizer of culture at large. Yet for decades after its invention in 1450, the press produced only a quantitative change (more books); limited marketplaces, limited travel, and limited literacy all conspired to thwart the invention's true potential. By contrast, we are immediately experiencing a

....

1. Elizabeth L. Eisenstein points out in *The Printing Press as an Agent of Change* that the sixteenth-century writer Michel de Montaigne had access to more books at his own home than earlier scholars could have encountered over a lifetime of global travels.

2. The meters and formulas of epic poetry were in fact memory aids that allowed for the recitation of extended narratives held entirely in the orator's mind. Karl Marx writes in *The German Ideology,* "Is it not inevitable that with the emergence of the press, the singing and the telling and the muse cease; that is, the conditions necessary for epic poetry disappear?"

3. History is littered with examples of technologies that multiply content and, in doing so, change the monopolies of knowledge in Europe and elsewhere. John Man writes about the Korean emperor Sejong, for example, who in 1443 introduced a simplified alphabet, Hangul, which appalled the elite of his country—they worked to block its proliferation. (See chapter 4 of Man's *The Gutenberg Revolution.*)

qualitative difference in our lives. Our fate is instantly and comprehensively reimagined by online technology.

For any single human to live through such a change is extraordinary. After all, the original Gutenberg shift in 1450 was not a *moment* that one person could have witnessed, but a slow-blooming *era* that took centuries before it was fully unpacked. Literacy in England was not common until the nineteenth century, so most folk until then had little direct contact with the printed book. And the printing machine itself was not fundamentally improved upon for the first 350 years of its existence.

But today: How quickly, how irrevocably, *this* kills *that.* Since ours is truly a single moment and not an era, scholars who specialize in fifteenth-century history may be able to make only partial comparisons with the landscape we're trekking through. While writing this book, I found it necessary to consult also with neuroscientists, psychiatrists, psychologists, technology gurus, literature professors, librarians, computer scientists, and more than a few random acquaintances who were willing to share their war stories. And all these folk, moving down their various roads, at last crossed paths—in that place called Absence. It was an idea of absence that seemed to come up time and again. Every expert, every scientist, and every friend I spoke with had a device in his or her pocket that could funnel a planet's worth of unabridged, incomprehensible clamor. Yet it was absence that unified the elegies I heard.

. . . . .

We may never comprehend just what was subsumed beneath the influence of Gutenberg's machine because the change was so total that it even became the screen through which we view the world. The gains the press yielded are mammoth and essential to our lives. But we forget: Every revolution in communication technology—from papyrus to the printing press to Twitter—is as much an opportunity to be drawn away from something as it is to be drawn toward something.

Marshall McLuhan wrote in *Understanding Media* that "a new medium is never an addition to an old one, nor does it leave the old one in peace." The successful new medium actively subjugates the older ones. It "never ceases to oppress the older media until it finds new shapes and positions for them." So the dismantling of magazine and newspaper offices, the vast fields of lost writers and editors now blogging and bitching from cafés around the world, are not just employment casualties; they're a symptom of a more profound wreckage.

As we embrace a technology's gifts, we usually fail to consider what they ask from us in return—the subtle, hardly noticeable payments we make in exchange for their marvelous service. We don't notice, for example, that the gaps in our schedules have disappeared because we're too busy delighting in the amusements that fill them. We forget the games that childhood boredom forged because boredom itself has been outlawed. Why would we bother to register the end of solitude, of ignorance, of lack? Why would we care that an absence has disappeared?

The more I thought about this seismic shift in our lives—our rapid movement toward online experience and away from rarer, concrete things—the more I wanted to understand the nature of the experience itself. How does it feel to live through our own Gutenberg moment? How does it *feel* to be the only people in history to know life with and without the Internet?

And if we work hard enough to understand this massive game changer, and then *name* the parts of the new game we want to go along with and the parts we don't, can we then pack along some critical aspect of our earlier lives that those technologies would otherwise strip from us? Or will we forget forever the value of that lack and instead see only a collection of gains? It's hard to remember what we loved about absence; we never ask for our deprivation back.

To understand our unique predicament, and understand how to win ourselves those best possible lives, we need to root out answers in every corner of our experience. But the questions we need to ask at each juncture remain as simple as they are urgent:

What will we carry forward?

And what worthy things might we thoughtlessly leave behind?

The answer to that second question was painfully clear as I sat at my little beige desk in the offices of *Vancouver* magazine. What I'd left behind was absence. As a storm of digital dispatches hammered at the wall of my computer screen, I found myself desperate for sanctuary. There was a revulsion against these patterns imposed on me. I wanted a long and empty wooden desk where I could get some real work done. I wanted a walk in the woods with nobody to meet. I wanted release from the migraine-scale pressure of constant communication, the ping-ping-ping of perma-messaging, the dominance of communication over experience.

Somehow I'd left behind my old quiet life. And now I wanted it back.

· · · · ·

If you were born before 1985, then you know what life is like both with the Internet and without. You are making the pilgrimage from Before to After. (Any younger and you haven't lived as an adult in a pre-Internet landscape.) Those of us in this straddle generation, with one foot in the digital pond and the other on the shore, are experiencing a strange suffering as we acclimatize. We are the digital immigrants, and like all immigrants, we don't always find the new world welcoming. The term itself—"digital immigrant"—isn't a perfect one: It's often assumed that the immigrant is somehow upgrading his or her citizenship or fleeing persecution. As for me and my peers, we may prefer to keep a pied-à-terre in the homeland of our youth.

Seen in a prudential light, our circumstances are also a tremendous gift. If we're the last people in history to know life before the Internet, we are also the only ones who will ever speak, as it were, both languages. We are the only fluent translators of Before and After. Our children will no more be able to see online life for what it is than we can comprehend the changes wrought by Gutenberg's printing press in the fifteenth century (or, for that matter, the changes our ancestors experienced when transitioning from an oral to a written culture). Some inventions are more than discreet gadgets; they dissolve into the very atmosphere of our lives. And who can notice the air?

. . . . .

Early on in my research for this book, I spoke with the celebrated cultural historian Alberto Manguel, who at the age of sixty-five largely eschews the bother of digital immigration. I wanted to hear in particular how this man, who wrote *A History of Reading,* felt about the movement toward digital text. "I can only describe it personally," he told me:

> For me the experience is one that is above all superficial. That is, the digital text has no physical reality for me. And it seems to require a certain urgency and speed, which is not what I look for when I'm reading.

Manguel encounters similar problems when writing with a digital device. On his computer, he feels constantly "conscious of the instrument I'm using. It always wants to be updated or somehow managed," while a pen is a comparatively neutral extension of his own body and mind. What's more, text on a computer always presents itself as though it were a finished work—the editing is invisible. "You don't see the history of the text," said Manguel. "This has a tragic side in that the texts written today appear to exist only in the presence of the reader, they have no past. We have eliminated the possibility of our books having biographies." But, like many in his age bracket, Manguel was quick to allow that such reservations are largely nostalgic, that qualms like his will not be felt by the next generation.

The end of such qualms, though, does not signify the loss of their value. Plenty of smart people have shuddered at new magnifiers of communication in ways that future generations would find quaint. Jean Cocteau thought the radio was a "faucet of foolishness" that was going to wreck people's minds. He wrote in his 1951 diary: "One wonders how a nation's intelligence resists the radio. Moreover it does not resist." Groucho Marx said he found television educational only because "every time someone switches it on, I go into the other room and read a book." And to Picasso, computers were useless since "they can only give you answers." While these complaints are outmoded and even naïve-looking today, I wouldn't call them invalid. For those of us who are buffeted by digital life, the antique tone of our discomfort is itself evidence that we're aware of the difference in a way that future generations won't be.

· · · · ·

If we maintain that cognizance of the difference between online life and offline life, we can choose to enjoy both worlds and move between them when we wish. This is no Sisyphean effort, either. Even as I began my research, there were intimations of change. Once an e-mail addict, I fled to my in-box less and less—finally settling on a maximum of three checks a day. I started leaving the house without thinking to grab the phone. And as I spoke about this book with friends, others spontaneously took up the challenge themselves.

Well, some did. Some, in fact, were offended by the pretense of my opting out. And that's fine. Not everyone feels there's a problem that needs correcting, after all. Not everyone feels this static. But for those who do feel it, there's a needful reaction that wells up. Perhaps, I thought, armed with the input of global experts and a little resolve, we can safeguard a vulnerable portion of our psyche.

That said, this book is not a wholesale critique of technology. Our technologies produce wonderful abbreviations, quickenings in our lives—and have done since our earliest ancestors looked down at their naked bodies and thought, Surely we can do better than this. Whether a wheel, or a condom, or a $150 billion International Space Station, our tools are brilliant extensions of human will; they shorten the distance between problem (that animal refuses to be eaten) and solution (smack him with my club). Our impulse to take up tools is a good one and—to use a deeply suspect term—it's a natural one. It's such a natural impulse, in fact, that those who question whether all technological developments will lead to brighter, happier futures are dismissed as Luddites. Interrogate the dominance of a mounting technopoly with anything more aggressive than cocktail conversation and you will swiftly be accused of "moral panic"—which is one of those tidy terms that carries around its own moral imperative. One *must not panic*.

Technologies themselves, though, are amoral. They aren't good or evil, only dangerous and beloved. They are a danger we've been in love with for millennia, and rarely do we remember that, for example, the goal of human relations may extend beyond efficient transmissions. (If we annihilate ourselves in the coming years, it will not be for lack of communication technology, though it may be for lack of some finer advancement.) Yet our devotion to tech-bolstered communication—to making common and shared as much of our lives as possible—often overwhelms us.

Consider the rapaciousness of our online activity. By 2012, we were asking Google to help us find things more than a trillion times each year (in a remarkable 146 languages). We were also sending one another 144 billion e-mails—every day. In 2013, we "liked" 4.5 billion items on Facebook every day, too (though boosterish Facebook still won't allow its users to dislike anything). That year, we uploaded one hundred hours of video to YouTube for every minute of real time. Every second, we uploaded 637 photos to Instagram. The content of our digital lives, in other words, has piled up into such significant forms that it can no longer be passed off as some appendage or decoration.

The breathtaking speed with which digital technologies draw close the world is reason enough to raise your eyebrows: In the past decade, Internet usage expanded 566 percent. Best estimates are that 40 percent of all people on the planet are now online. Social media trains our behavior en masse—half of Internet users connect with friends and family on Facebook, as do 59 percent of online Americans (and 93 percent of college students). I do not, and I am consequently left in the dark about things as essential as weddings, moves, births, and deaths. In Malaysia, where Linda from our prologue hails from, Facebook has now achieved a penetration rate of more than 70 percent among Internet users (apparently because the app allows for cheaper messaging).

The sheer volume of time we devote to our devices means we each are carving "expendable" hours away from other parts of our lives. We rationalize the interruptions that our phones and tablets demand—each checking of e-mail or scanning of YouTube is, after all, just a momentary concession. But in each month of 2012, Americans spent 520 billion of those simple minutes connecting to the Internet on their devices. That's nearly 100 billion more minutes every month than the previous year.

Nor is this change a mere ballooning of what came before. Like writing, clocks, and the printing press, the Internet and its cronies are indiscriminate game changers. They don't just enrich our experiences; they *become* our experiences. This is something Susan Greenfield, a professor of synaptic pharmacology at Oxford University, spoke about recently when being interviewed by *The New York Times*:

> A car or a plane enabled you to travel farther and faster. What concerns me is that the current technologies have been converted from being means to being ends. [The Internet] seems to have become an end in and of itself.

And how might we describe that end? So much of our inventiveness, it turns out, wells up from, and then perpetuates, a deep desire to gather the world into our arms. The harnessing of magnetism leads to the compass, making expansive seafaring possible. James Watt's invention of the modern steam engine in 1765 obliterates distance. The telegraph, the transatlantic cable, and the telephone cast larger and larger lassos to draw home the voices of faraway lovers, peers, and purveyors of news. Motion pictures, at the end of the nineteenth century, reap a world's worth of glittering images and deliver them to enthralled viewers in the dark.

We crowded the world into our small lives. And the crowding claimed its victims.

· · · · ·

In Victor Hugo's *Notre-Dame de Paris* (which is set in 1482, when printing presses were just getting established in Louis XI's France), Archdeacon Claude Frollo sees his first printed book and marvels/glowers at its production quality. He stands near Notre-Dame and, looking up at the cathedral, says, *"Ceci tuera cela"* ("This will kill that"). How does a book kill a cathedral? We're speaking in synecdoche here: The printing press (engine of democracy, aid to Martin Luther) will kill the Catholic Church.

Also, more literally, the printed book became a nimbler conveyer of meaning than grand architectural gestures (like Notre-Dame), which had stood for millennia as "the great handwriting of the human race." The printed word disrupts not just the standard hierarchy of information transmission, but a *way* of knowing that's sacred and beyond the handlings of everyday folk. Of course, from Hugo's vantage point—his novel was published in 1831—he could give Frollo a degree of foresight that would have been lacking in an honest citizen of fifteenth-century Paris.

Living in the real maelstrom of change, however, means blindness. And so the details of our own Gutenberg moment remain partly obscure. But this much we know: Just as every technology is an invitation to enhance some part of our lives, it's also, necessarily, an invitation to be drawn away from something else. The things we're glad to be drawn away from (dying of exposure, Black Death) are easier to remember than the things we might have wanted to hold on to (rural life, restful mornings). The more I thought about our Gutenberg moment, the more I wondered: Drawn away from what? What is this feeling of mysterious loss that hits us each step down that path? I kept coming back to the loss of lack, the end of absence.

Just two decades beyond the Internet's popularization, we've no hope of seeing our lives as clearly as Victor Hugo saw Frollo's. For an author writing in 2350, the defining features of our time will be evident (or boiled down, anyway, by the reductive powers of historians), and the consequences of online migration will undoubtedly include by-products we cannot now predict. Certainly we—floating among the flotsam of our own exploded reality—cannot yet list everything the Internet has tampered with. But stand in Times Square sometime and look up from a glowing iPad at the New York Times building (where hundreds of positions have been cut in recent years). We can already say, *"Ceci tuera cela."* And although confident future historians may deliver a clear picture of this revolution we're living through, those of us alive today—we in the straddle generation—have a secret bit of understanding they can never have: We know what it felt like Before.

. . . . .

We carry around in our heads the final version of certain stories. Like this one:

I remember that final blithe summer of 1999 when I—like so many others—embarked on the last trip I'd ever take without a cell phone. Hiking for months through England's Lake District and island hopping across the Scottish Hebrides, I was oblivious to the fact that I would never experience such splendid isolation again. Never again would I be so completely cut off from work, from family, from friends. And yet, nineteen years old and living happily off apples and beer, I didn't think it was the end of anything. So, I told myself, this is my life at last, the beginning of my real life.

I was in league, in my little way, with Henry David Thoreau:

Not till we are lost, in other words, not till we have lost the world, do we begin to find ourselves, and realize where we are and the infinite extent of our relations.

Like Thoreau, and like any number of young people who then would trek out after high school with no guide but the *Lonely Planet* in their pack, I wanted to get lost. I was in search of absence. I felt that it wasn't networking I needed, but a connection to some deep source that I could not describe for myself yet intuitively felt was there beyond the busy prescriptions of school. My days were largely filled with walks down silent paths and across wild fields I never knew the names for. In the evenings, I would discuss movies and politics with strangers at some village pub, then happily tramp across a darkening sea of heather.

That heather—the hills and hills of its rustling color. One

night, a man with a craggy face invited me to stay on and learn to make thatched roofs from the stuff, be his apprentice, spend my life picking heather in the morning and weaving it into watertight mats in the afternoon. At two in the morning I told him I would; but by dawn my saner self took over, and I left for Heathrow and home.

Flip forward fourteen years. . . . Today, the world's atmosphere heaves with signals from more than six billion cell phones. I'm writing these words on a worn wooden bench in a train station's lounge in the Canadian city of Winnipeg. I'm chewing on a Styrofoam cup of coffee, scratching at a head of graying hair. Across from me are four teenagers in depressingly expensive T-shirts, making furious use of the two-hour e-mail break we have, here in the city. (I elected to train across the country, sampling brief patches of Internet abstinence in the signal-free wildernesses of Canada's glacial mountains and staring plains.) These kids are all about the age I was when I first had a broken heart, when my hair was chestnut brown and I might have become a heather picker. They mumble to one another, friendly enough, but mostly it is their phones that grip their various attentions.

According to research by Nielsen, the average teenager now manages upward of four thousand text messages every month, so these youths sitting before me must work fast, I suppose, to reach their daily quota. What strikes me, though, is the utter solicitude with which they grip at, gaze at, graze at, their devices. It is the sort of rapt attention normally reserved for babes in arms. Certainly older people may spend half their lives in similar thrall, but I've been thinking about my halcyon days in the British countryside this morning, so the phone-leashed youths make me wince.

I think of the lives these digital natives—who have known nothing but an online world—are crafting for themselves, the lives that are being crafted for them. These youths, as bright and eager and ready for life as we all were, have the opportunity to inhabit two worlds: one digital, one corporeal; they could transit between the two. But I wonder which they will cling to as life barrels over them—when they fall in love, when they lose a parent. And which world might they let go of? Young and old, we're all straddling two realities to a certain degree. In our rush toward the promise of Google and Facebook—toward the promise of reduced ignorance and reduced loneliness—we feel certain we are rushing toward a better life. We forget the myriad accommodations we made along the way.

An announcement echoes senselessly around the train station, and one of the teenagers looks up from her phone; she catches me staring. She holds my gaze for a moment, with the narrowing expression of a woman who is used to being looked at. I smile across the lounge and she rolls her eyes, as though to say, "You *wish*." She returns to her phone.

CHAPTER 2
Kids These Days

Human brains are exquisitely evolved to adapt to the environment in which they're placed. It follows that if the environment is changing in an unprecedented way, then the changes too will be unprecedented. . . . So the fear I have is not with the technology per se, but the way it's used by the native mind.

—Susan Greenfield in *The New York Times*

I find myself at that troubling time of life when one's friends proceed—without asking permission—to have children. These offspring are pleasant and worthwhile things, I'm sure, but they're also expert dismantlers of conversation. I'm speaking here of the sustained and "deep" conversations my group thought we would continue to enjoy long after the conclusion of our university days. Only five years ago, we would stay up late drinking bad coffee and arguing about the banality of evil. Tonight, after a brisk dinner of pasta at one friend's home, I find myself on the floor with a couple of toddlers, debating the relative merits of *My Little Pony*. The rest of the party is also grounded. We are reduced to the common denominator of infanthood. We pass toy trucks to the children, receive discarded socks in return, quaff some half-decent Shiraz, and end up, inevitably, lying on our bellies trying to wrest the attention of an infant away from his iPad. The tablet glows and we do not.

I was amazed the other night to discover that the iPad is a sedative as well as a stimulant. My nephew Benjamin was fussing at a restaurant until his father produced the tablet from a diaper bag and placed it before his son: instant calm. I silently disapproved of the tactic, as only the childless could. And his dad gave me a guilty shrug as if to say, "It's awful, but it works." We carried on with our dinner in peace. (The iPad works as a laxative, too: CTA Digital released its iPotty in 2013, a toilet for toddlers with a stand for their tablets, to ensure entertaining poops.)

Tonight, young Benjamin falls upon a print magazine that has been abandoned on the floor (a chunky issue of *Vanity Fair*). I watch his two-year-old eyes scan the glossy cover, which shines less fiercely than the iPad he is used to but has a faint luster of its own. And then I watch his pudgy thumb and index finger pinch together and spread apart on Bradley Cooper's smiling mug. He continues this action a few times, and it dawns on me that he's attempting to zoom in. At last, Benjamin looks over at me, flummoxed and frustrated, as though to say, "This thing's broken."

At thirty-three, I suddenly find myself positioned against "kids these days." To my disappointment, the sentiment smacks only a little of self-satisfaction; mostly it feels like informed foreboding. *Kids these days,* I hear myself say in an ironic interior voice. And then I realize I don't feel ironic about the sentiment at all. "Kids these days," I say out loud, taking the magazine from under Benjamin's arm and slowly, manually, turning the pages for him.

It was one of those *no, really* moments. No, really, this child is a step away from assuming that the world is one cohesive digital technology; one step away from assuming that such technology is inherent in the material world—a natural, spontaneous part of it. He'll grow up thinking about the Internet with the same nonchalance that I hold toward my toaster and teakettle. Why shouldn't he think of these technologies as a constant, a given, when he has been bathed so persistently in the cool electric glow of LED light?

Back at home, my partner, Kenny, wisely pads off to bed as I stay up, discovering a slew of videos online featuring babies and toddlers experiencing the same confusion as Benjamin. Search YouTube for "baby" and "iPad" and you'll find clips featuring one-year-olds attempting to manipulate magazine pages and television screens as though they were touch-sensitive displays. And this with hands that cannot yet grip a crayon. Of *course* toddlers think everything's touch-sensitive, says Kenny the next morning over cereal. Our brains are engineered to work with assumptions about the tools we use. A plastic switch is always going to activate a lightbulb when flicked; a window will safely slide open when pushed. If our brains didn't make these assumptions, he reminds me, we wouldn't get very far.

I sigh for effect, wondering about Kenny's neuroscience credentials, and outside the window, on cue, a set of phone-leashed children go marching softly by. I can resist all I like, but for Benjamin's generation resistance is moot. The revolution is already complete.

·　·　·　·　·

Naturally, the young lead the charge. As early as 2010, the Kaiser Foundation found that eight- to eighteen-year-olds were devoting seven hours and thirty-eight minutes each day to their devices. Of course those youths, expert multitaskers, are often consuming more than one media at a time; when teens work on their homework, in fact, a full two-thirds of them are multitasking. If need be, they can simultaneously text, watch music videos, groom their Facebook page, and play *Call of Duty,* all while polishing up an essay on *Hamlet.* All told, at least 29 percent of media exposure among teenagers involves multitasking. (That most dubious of digital age virtues is looked at more closely in chapter 6.) When this multitasking is accounted for, the media consumption rate among youths rises to a total of ten hours and forty-five minutes each day. Five years earlier, that number sat at eight hours and thirty-three minutes; five years before that, it was seven hours and twenty-nine minutes. The difference in activity between one generation and the next is stark: Nielsen research from 2013 found that the average American adult sends and receives 764 text messages each month, a fraction of the several thousand managed by their teenage children. There is, though, one kind of media that youths are consuming less of. Printed books, magazines, and newspapers are dropping from their hands. It is the sole form of media consumption that is waning.[4]

The numbers are impressive. However, to really see how kids resort to their devices, you need to stake out a miserable, badly lit environment where they're trapped and bored. A doctor's office works. But buses are my preferred observational venue. Today I rode one from downtown Vancouver to the suburbs and had an excellent sighting. One boy—perhaps sixteen years old—was sitting, broad-legged and depressed, staring into his own crotch, where he gripped his little glowing phone. When another teenager boarded the bus and sat opposite the first, it was clear that this new youth recognized the other. He smiled at the boy for a moment but then, unable to gain his attention, returned his gaze to his own phone. I watched (slyly, I hope) while the two boys proceeded to message each other, back and forth, for the remainder of their bus ride. About halfway through this engagement, the first boy looked up from a text and laughed at the

....

4. The Kaiser Foundation's latest numbers tell us that print consumption, outside of reading for school, takes up an average of thirty-eight minutes in every youth's day (a small but telling drop from forty-three minutes five years earlier).

second boy, who had clearly just texted a "reveal" to the first. But the pair did not proceed to have a face-to-face conversation after this revelation. They reverted to their phones and kept texting back and forth, occasionally giggling and offering shy smiles at each other across the aisle. When we don't want to be alone and yet don't want the hassle that fellow humans represent either, the digital filter is an ideal compromise.

Another telling bus sighting: two girls sharing earbuds as they travel. They smile, share their music, play videos for each other; the phone becomes an intersection for their mutual affection. Like the boys, these girls enjoy a constant connection while their device serves as the ultimate party host, the ultimate bonding agent. Have these people found ways to expand their understanding, reduce their estrangement, and produce happier, more fulfilled lives? Or have they simply accommodated themselves to their void-filling tools?

· · · · ·

The smartphone is itself a far, far safer friend than a messy, unpredictable human. Far less frightening to deal with and less likely to suffer from mood swings or halitosis. Our solicitous relationship with our phones can seem a creepy kind of attachment, but we forget that this tender love for handheld electronics is not so new a thing. We've been bonding in truly affectionate ways with interactive computers for decades. In the late 1990s, robotic creatures called Tamagotchis and Furbies were sold to tens of millions of children. I myself played chess with a robotic chessboard in my lonely bedroom as a child (and was duly gratified by its lack of gloating each time it bested me), but I was just old enough to miss the wave of truly compelling robo-friends. Part of me wonders whether it was this dodge that left me feeling so different from people even a few years younger than me. My younger cousins all carried Tamagotchis and Furbies to school; they

constantly monitored what, at the time, seemed to be sophisticated, emotional machines that begged for care and got it. (Hold
a Furby upside down and it will cry, "Me scared!") Much as I
liked my automatic chessboard, I never learned to love it.

Sherry Turkle, the director of MIT's Initiative on Technology
and Self, documents hundreds of interviews with children who
have bonded with robots and other technologies in her book
Alone Together. She paints a compelling picture of an emerging
population more at ease with technologies than with one another.
The phone is easy, people are hard. But even then, it's texting that
is acceptable since voice-to-voice phone conversations have too
many potential pitfalls. Text messages, even if they lack subtle
intonation, are discreet and controllable. And that's a trade-off
we're eager to make. "We have to be concerned," Turkle concludes, "that the simplification and reduction of relationship is no
longer something we complain about. It may become what we
expect, even desire."

And how we do desire those reductions. As our phones ban-
ish the wide-open possibilities of boredom, they deliver a strict
context that lets us moor ourselves in an ocean of distraction
that would otherwise drown us. Those teenage boys on the bus
have found in their phones some intense friendships, but with
the kinds of friends that demand obedience. Our "contacts" become ordered by the phone's own software, and the portal to
those ordered contacts (as opposed to actual people) becomes a
larger locus of attention. Perhaps this abstracting of "contacts"
is reflective of a larger shift? A University of Michigan metastudy
released in the summer of 2010 compiled data from seventy-two
studies conducted between 1979 and 2009, all geared toward
monitoring levels of empathy among American college students;
the metastudy found that today's youths were scoring 40 percent
lower than their earlier counterparts. Meanwhile, a 2013 metastudy out of San Diego University demonstrated increased levels
of narcissism among youths. Certainly I've found that my own

contact with friends becomes increasingly impersonal and less empathetic the more it's filtered through the reductive emoticons and textual abbreviations of my phone.

When I consider the interpersonal skills inherent in digital natives who multitask a third of the time they're supposed to be focusing on something, it often strikes me that the elder generation has enormous advantages. In my arrogance, I think to myself that nobody would want to hire an individual incapable of thinking in full sentences. The only significant advantage left to the young will be their youthful looks—their sex appeal—for which an older population will forgive very much. This, I tell myself with a shot of glee, will fade. And then what will a constantly distracted fifty-year-old really bring to the table, except a facility with the technology that made him or her that way? But that, of course, is a fantasy; that fifty-year-old will be a multitasker in a multitasking world. And my own idea of a work ethic will be outmoded.

No two generations in history have experienced such a highlighted cognitive dissonance, because never has change occurred at so rapid a pace. Look at the rate of penetration—the amount of time it takes for a new technology to be adopted by fifty million people. Radio took thirty-eight years to reach that mark; the telephone took twenty years; and television took thirteen. More recently, the World Wide Web took four years, Facebook took 3.6, Twitter took three, and the iPad took only two. Google Plus, which nobody even finds useful, took only eighty-eight days to be adopted by fifty million. The rate of technology absorption is stunning: Just one generation after the first cell phone call took place (in 1973), there are now 6.8 billion cell phone subscriptions— nearing a 1:1 ratio with human beings. In South Korea, that number reaches a sobering 99 percent saturation. In some countries— Russia, China, and Brazil, for example—a third of the population maintains two cell phones. And in China (in a bid either for compartmentalized lives or to take advantage of multiple billing plans), a committed 6 percent of the population maintains three or more phones at all times.

What we're witnessing is a kind of instant complicity, a massive and swift behavior shift. And so it may come to pass that a person disconnected from (or merely disinterested in) this flood of new technologies could, in a few years, be made entirely alien to a younger generation. Step out of a running stream and you cannot reenter the same water. I myself stepped away from video games for a decade and now I'm unable to reenter the fray. The latest games are nonsensical and manic to me, though people older than me—who never stepped out of the stream—are perfectly at ease, even thrilled, with the latest offerings.

. . . . .

Wariness about the way our technologies are shaping our thoughts, mutterings about "kids these days" and their gadgets, can be tracked back thousands of years. Most famous among the cranks is kindly Socrates, who was perhaps the first to wonder whether gadgets—in his case *letters* and *writing*—could change mental processes.

In Plato's *Phaedrus*, we hear Socrates describing how a king from Egypt called Thamus informed the god Theuth that the phonetic alphabet was not so great a gift. The god was particularly chuffed about this new technology, which he delivered to poor, illiterate humans, bragging that writing would make the memories of Egyptians more powerful and that it would supercharge their wit. King Thamus shrewdly replies:

> O most ingenious Theuth . . . this discovery of yours will create forgetfulness in the learners' souls, because they will not use their memories; they will trust to the external written characters and not remember of themselves. The specific which you have discovered is an aid

not to memory, but to reminiscence, and you give your
disciples not truth, but only the semblance of truth; they
will be hearers of many things and will have learned
nothing; they will appear to be omniscient and will generally know nothing.

Was there ever a finer description of Google? "An aid not to
memory, but to reminiscence." Real memory and the magic trick
of reminiscence, of course, are not the same thing at all. We reminisce when something external recalls the memory for us. Unlike our hard-won memories, a reminiscence is easy, passive, and
provided by some reminder. But the user of a technology that
recollects on his or her behalf (a scroll, say, stuffed with important dates and names) is not likely to care about that subtle distinction. Kids these days, for Socrates, were rotting their brains
by abandoning the oral tradition.

Several millennia later, in the fifteenth century, the fantasti-
cally named Venetian editor Hieronimo Squarciafico looked
around at "kids these days" and groaned that the advent of book
publishing would lead to intellectual laziness. Men would become less studious when material became so cheap to produce
and so whorishly available. The mind would turn to mush. The
Florentine book merchant Vespasiano da Bisticci backed Squarciafico up, saying that a printed book should be "ashamed" in
the company of a handmade manuscript (one wonders whether
his disdain was motivated more by business concerns than aes-
thetics).

Our modern, studious commitment to the technologies of
writing and printing, then, is a startling departure from the experience of our ancestors. Those men weren't wrong to be suspicious; something fundamental *had* been changed. Here's Berkeley
psychologist Alison Gopnik, describing how the act of reading
reshaped our brains long before the Internet got its hands on
them:

Cortical areas that once were devoted to vision and speech have been hijacked by print. Instead of learning through practice and apprenticeship, I've become dependent on lectures and textbooks. And look at the toll of dyslexia and attention disorders and learning disabilities—all signs that our brains were not designed to deal with such a profoundly unnatural technology.

Our devotion to reading feels wholesome, natural, but is in fact a wonderful kind of brainwashing. Marshall McLuhan, having fewer brain scans in his arsenal than Gopnik, speaks in more obscure terms when analyzing the fallout of the printing press. For him, printed words became a gravitational force, something our minds reorganized around. "For the most obvious character of print," he notes, "is repetition, just as the obvious effect of repetition is hypnosis or obsession." For McLuhan, Stephen King novels and ingredients lists on cereal boxes and the words you're reading right now are all conspiring to make you think this strange attention you're paying to tiny lines of printed symbols is a natural act. But it's not. The intensely myopic attention that the act of poring over a book requires of us is anything but natural, and it reshaped our attitude toward the world at large, bringing about—according to McLuhan—the dawn of capitalism, the regulation of language, and the dominance of the visual at the expense of our multisensory lives: "The eye speeded up and the voice quieted down." He attributes the bulk of our "shrill and expansive individualism" to Gutenberg's invention.

After the arrival of mass-produced books, we became "typographical man," and our voices lost some power. We were encouraged by the technologies of writing and printing to take on some kinds of input and discouraged from taking on others. Today we privilege the information we take in through our eyes while reading and pay less heed to information that arrives via our other senses. In plainest terms, McLuhan delivers his famous line: "The medium is the message." What you use to interact with the world changes the way you see the world. Every lens is a tinted lens.

· · · · ·

A latter-day King Thamus or Squarciafico would grumble at me for using my phone to call up my partner's number. In fact, I've never known Kenny's number by heart. But it's not something I worry about or seek to fix. Likewise, if adults in 2064 manage to entirely outsource their memories to digital aids, they won't begrudge their situation at all, but will rejoice in their mental freedom. How many of us long for more things to store in our brains? Indeed, the value of doing things the hard way becomes a question of "things you never knew you never knew," to steal a line from Disney's *Pocahontas*. I don't know what satisfaction I might gain from carrying that information in my brain instead, just as my child will never know the value of learning to read a map without GPS. And neither of us will think to care. This is the problem with losing lack: It's nearly impossible to recall its value once it's gone.

Which is why the ancients all cry out in their turn: "Kids these days!" Youths, and the technologies that inform their sensibilities, will always be at odds with the dying techno-sensibility that informed the character of their elders. Yet the scale of discordance in contemporary culture is perhaps an unprecedented thing. Digital natives are subject to a violent removal from the habits of their parents, a shift that will leave them quite alien to those only one generation older, and vice versa.

When I pause to consider that last remark, I see I'm being way too conservative. There's actually a chasm between me and folk *five* years younger. The other day, I was speaking with a young friend of mine—a journalist in his late twenties—and he thought nothing of carrying on a text conversation with someone else while speaking with me. (I am, trust me, painfully aware of being transformed into the kind of man people call "crotchety" here.) It's a common annoyance, barely worth noting, except that I'd been thinking about what it meant to be constantly put on hold by a person I'm sharing a beer with. It seemed to me that 80 percent of his attention procured 20 percent of my interest. It's a case of compound distraction. But the really gruesome thing was that he didn't notice or care that we were both so disengaged. The "natural" attention of someone just a few years younger than me is vastly more kinetic and fractured—attention span has evolved.

Just how insidious is our difference in attitude? How violent is the change between one mental state and the next?

· · · · ·

The brains our children are born with are not substantively different from the brains our ancestors were born with forty thousand years ago. For all the wild variety of our cultures, personalities, and thought patterns, we're all still operating with roughly the same three-pound lump of gray jelly. But almost from day one, the allotment of those brains (and therefore the way they function) is different today from the way it was even one generation ago. Every second of your lived experience represents new connections among the roughly eighty-six billion neurons packed inside your brain. Every minute you spend in the particular world that you were born into makes you massively, and functionally, different from those who came before. Children, then, can become literally incapable of thinking and feeling the way their grandparents did. A slower, less harried way of thinking may be on the verge of extinction.

To understand the severity of this predicament, though, we first need to understand just how very vulnerable, how plastic, our minds really are.

The plasticity of our minds is a marvelous thing to behold.

In your brain alone, your billions of neurons are tied to each other by trillions of synapses, a portion of which are firing right now, forging (by still mysterious means) your memory of this sentence, your critique of this very notion, and your emotions as you reflect on this information. And these transmissions play out, we're finding, in a highly organic and malleable fashion. Our brains are so plastic, so open-minded, that they will reengineer themselves to function optimally in whatever environment we give them. Repetition of stimuli produces a strengthening of responding neural circuits. Neglect of other stimuli will cause corresponding neural circuits to weaken. (Grannies who maintain their crossword puzzle regime knew that already.)

And as crossword-puzzling grandmothers know, it is not only the brains of the young that are vulnerable to environmental influence. While many still think that our personalities—and our brains—effectively crystallize when we graduate high school, we now know that our brains in fact remain plastic, changeable, throughout our lives. No matter your age, your brain's ability to think, to feel, to learn, is minutely different from the way it was yesterday. What you think and how you think are up for grabs.

This plasticity is the ultimate consolation for the perennial "nature vs. nurture" argument, by the way. Evolution (nature) endowed us with minds capable of fast and furious transformation, minds able to adapt to strange new environments (nurture) within a single lifetime—even within a few weeks. Therefore, we're always products of both inherited hardware and recently downloaded software. We are each a brilliant symbiosis of nature *and* nurture.

UCLA's Gary Small is a pioneer of neuroplasticity research, and in 2008 he produced the first solid evidence showing that our brains are reorganized by our use of the Internet. He placed a set of "Internet naïve" people in MRI machines and made recordings of their brain activity while they took a stab at going online. Small then had each of them practice browsing the

Internet for an hour a day for a mere week. On returning to the MRI machine, those "naïve" folk now toted brains that lit up significantly in the frontal lobe, where there had been minimal neural activity beforehand. Neural pathways quickly develop when we give our brains new tasks, and Small had shown that this held true—over the course of just a few hours, in fact—following Internet use.

"We know that technology is changing our lives. It's also changing our brains," he announced. On the one hand, neuroplasticity gives him great hope for the elderly. "It's not just some linear trajectory with older brains getting weaker," he told me. Your brain's ability to empathize, for example, will increase as you age. The flip side of all this, though, is that young brains, immersed in a dozen hours of screen time a day, may be more equipped to deal with digital reality than with the decidedly less flashy *reality* reality that makes up our dirty, sometimes boring, often quiet, material world.

In *The Shallows*, Nicholas Carr describes how the Internet fundamentally works on our plastic minds to make them more capable of "shallow" thinking and less capable of "deep" thinking. After enough time in front of our screens, we learn to absorb more information less effectively, skip the bottom half of paragraphs, shift focus constantly; "the brighter the software, the dimmer the user," he suggests at one point.

The most startling example of our brain's malleability, though, comes from new research by neural engineers who now suggest that our children will be able to "incept" a person "to acquire new learning, skills, or memory, or possibly restore skills or knowledge that has been damaged through accident, disease, or aging, without a person's awareness of what is learned or memorized." I am quoting here from a report issued from a Boston University team led by Takeo Watanabe. His team was able to use decoded functional magnetic resonance imaging (fMRI) to modify in highly specific ways the brain activity in the visual cortex of their human subjects. "Think of a person watching a computer screen," suggested the National Science Foundation when it announced the research, "and having his or her brain patterns modified to match those of a high-performing athlete." The possibilities of such injections of "unearned" learning are as marvelous as they are quagmires for bioethical debate. Your grandchild's brain could be trained in a certain direction while watching ads through digital contact lenses without his or her awareness (or, for that matter, acquiescence). In other words, decoded neurofeedback promises truly passive learning, learning without intention from the person who is to be "informed."

For now, it's easier to tell that something has changed in our minds, but we still feel helpless against it, and we even feel addicted to the technologies that are that change's agents.

But will our children feel the static? Will *X Factor* audition videos replace basement jam sessions? Will "deep" conversation and solitary walks be replaced by an impoverished experience of text clouds? Will the soft certainty of earlier childhood be replaced by the restless idleness that now encroaches? Our children will always have their moments of absence, of course—their lives will not be wholly zombielike but will be a mixture of connection and disconnection. They will get lost in the woods, they will run naked on beaches, they will sometimes shut off their devices. The important question is whether the bias is shifting—whether they'll find it as easy to access absence and solitude. What's important is that we become responsible for the media diets of our children in a way that past generations never were. Since our children are privy to a superabundance of media, we now need to proactively engineer moments of absence for them. We cannot afford to count on accidental absence any more than we can count on accidental veggies at dinner.

Without such engineered absences (a weekend without texting, a night without screens), our children suffer as surely as do kids with endless access to fast food. The result is a digital native population that's less well rounded than we know they could be. In 2012, Elon University worked with the Pew Internet and American Life Project to release a report that compiled the opinions of 1,021 critics, experts, and stakeholders, asking for their thoughts on digital natives. Their boiled-down message was that young people now count on the Internet as "their external brain" and have become skillful decision makers—even while they also "thirst for instant gratification and often make quick, shallow choices." Some of those experts were optimistic about the future brains of the young. Susan Price, CEO and chief Web strategist at San Antonio's Firecat Studio, suggested that "those who bemoan the perceived decline in deep thinking . . . fail to appreciate the need to evolve our processes and behaviors to suit the new realities and opportunities." Price promises that the young (and those who are young at heart) are developing new skills and standards better suited to their own reality than to the outmoded reality of, say, 1992.

Those "new standards" may, one presumes, place a priority on the processing of information rather than the actual absorption of information. In Socrates' terms, we're talking about reminiscence instead of memory, and the appearance of omniscience. Meanwhile, the report's coauthor, Janna Anderson, noted that while many respondents were enthusiastic about the future of such minds, there was a clear dissenting voice:

> Some said they are already witnessing deficiencies in young people's abilities to focus their attention, be patient and think deeply. Some experts expressed concerns that trends are leading to a future in which most people become shallow consumers of information, endangering society.

Several respondents took the opportunity, in fact, to cite George Orwell's dystopian fantasy 1984. Citizens are always manipulated by some authority or other, but an Orwellian future all but wipes out consciousness of (and criticism of) the subjugation of the masses. In order to keep youths noticing those manipulations in our own pseudo-Orwellian world, we first need to teach them how our technologies evolved.

· · · · ·

Charles Darwin's *The Origin of Species* may have outlined, back in 1859, an idea that explains our children's relationship with iPhones and Facebook. Here's the elevator-pitch version of his book: If you have something that copies itself with slight variations, and if that something exists in a competitive environment that will weed out those less suited to the given environment, then you must get what the American philosopher Daniel Dennett has called "design out of chaos without the aid of mind." Evolution is not, then, some magical occurrence, but a mathematical certainty. Given an item's ability to copy itself with variation, and given a competitive environment, you *must* have evolution.

So is the goop of our DNA the only thing in the universe that can meet Darwin's requirements for evolution? The English evolutionary biologist Richard Dawkins took the next logical step in 1976 and coined one of the most important, misunderstood, and bandied-about terms of our age: the meme.

The "meme" (from the ancient Greek *mimeme*, which means "that which is imitated") is an extension of Darwin's Big Idea past the boundaries of genetics. A meme, put simply, is a cultural product that is copied. A tune is one; so is a corporate logo, a style of dress, or a literary cliché like "the hero's journey." We humans are enamored of imitation and so become the ultimate "meme machines." The young are best of all: Twerking videos and sleepover selfies are memes par excellence. Memes—pieces of culture—copy themselves through history and enjoy a kind of evolution of their own, and they do so riding on the backs of successful genes: ours.

Our genes and memes have been working to shape us since humans first started copying one another's raw vocalizations. But now we may be witness to a third kind of evolution, one played out by our technologies. This new evolution is posited not by a Silicon Valley teen, but by a sixty-one-year-old woman in rural England named Susan Blackmore. Just as Darwinism submits that genes good at replicating will naturally become the most prevalent, Blackmore submits that technologies with a knack for replication will obviously rise to dominance. These "temes," as she's called these new replicators, could be copied, varied, and selected as digital information—thus establishing a new evolutionary process (and one far speedier than our genetic model). Evolutionary theory holds that given a million technological efforts, some are bound to be better at making us addicted to them, and these give rise, organically (as it were), to more and more addictive technologies, leaving each generation of humans increasingly in service to, and in thrall of, inanimate entities. Until we end up . . . well, where we are.

Blackmore's work offers a fascinating explanation for why each generation seems less and less capable of managing that solitude, less likely to opt for technological disengagement. She suggests that technology-based memes—temes—are a different kind of replicator from the basic memes of everyday material culture, the ones Dawkins was describing. What sort of difference is there? I wanted to know. "The most important difference is the fidelity of copying," she told me. This is important because a meme's ability to propagate grows as its fidelity rate increases. "Most memes . . . we forget how often we get them wrong." (Oral traditions of storytelling, for example, were characterized by constant twists in the tale.) "But with digital machines the fidelity is almost 100 percent. As it is, indeed, with our genes." This is a startling thought, though a simple enough one: By delivering to the world technologies capable of replicating information with the same accuracy as DNA, we are playing a grand game indeed. The fidelity of our earliest memetic acts would have improved significantly with the advent of writing, of course, and then again thanks to the printing press, which might (like us) be called a meme machine. But we now have near perfect replication online.

We are now becoming, by Blackmore's estimation, teme machines—servants to the evolution of our own technologies. The power shifts very quickly from the spark of human intention to the absorption of human will by a technology that seems to have intentions of its own.

Kevin Kelly takes this notion to the nth degree in his 2010 book, *What Technology Wants*, where he anthropomorphizes technologies and asks what they would like us to do. "The evolution of technology converges in much the same manner as biological evolution," he argues. He sees parallels to bioevolution in the fact that the number of lines of code in Microsoft Windows, for example, multiplied ten times since 1993, becoming more complex as time goes on just as biological organisms tend to do.

But viewed in the clear light of morning, we'll likely find there was no robotic villain behind the curtain. Your iPhone does not "want" anything in the way that we perceive "want" to exist. Instead of animal "want," we will confront only the cool, unthinking intelligence of evolution's law. And, to be sure, our own capitalist drive pushes these technologies, these temes, to evolve (if that's what they're doing). Consider the fact that Google tested forty-one shades of blue on its toolbar to see which elicited the most favorable response. We *push* the technology down an evolutionary path that results in the most addictive possible outcome. Yet even as we do this, it doesn't feel as though we have any control. It feels, instead, like a destined outcome—a fate.

· · · · ·

Blackmore's conception, if thrilling, is also harrowing. Genes must cooperate with us to get copied into the next generation, and they produce animals that cooperate with one another. And temes (being bits of information, not sentient creatures) need humans to build the factories and servers that allow them to replicate, and they need us to supply the power that runs the machines. But as temes evolve, they could demand more than a few servers from future generations of humans. Blackmore continued:

> What really scares me is that the accelerating evolution of temes and their machinery requires vast amounts of energy and material resources. We will go on supplying these as long as we want to use the technology, and it will adapt to provide us what we want while massively expanding of its own accord. Destruction of the climate and of earth's ecosystems is the inevitable outlook. It is this that worries me—not whether they are amoral or not.

Blackmore's vision for our children's technological future may seem nightmarish to the point of fantasy, especially since she seems to be constantly reporting the future, suggesting eventualities that cannot be determined the way we like.

Yet when I think now of all that Blackmore told me, and of the eerie promise of decoded neurofeedback, when I think of the advancing multitudes of youths (and adults, too) who seem so perilously entranced by inanimate tools, I do sometimes lose heart. Then again, I want to counter all that with an opposing vision.

The best way I can describe this optimistic alternative is to call up a scene from that 1999 gem of a movie *The Matrix*. In the Wachowski siblings' film, a population enslaved by computers has been turned into a warehouse of mere battery cells, kept complacent by a mass delusion, the Matrix, which is fed into human brains and keeps them thinking they are living their own lives, freely, on the sunny streets of the world. In fact, as they dream out their false experiences, their physical bodies are held in subterranean caverns, each sleeping human jacked into a womblike pod. In my favorite scene, Neo, our hero, is torn from this dreamworld and awakens in that great dark chamber. Gasping for air, the first real air he has ever breathed, Neo stares out with stunned eyes and sees the raw world at last.[5]

The Matrix is a technologically derived web of illusions, a computer-generated dreamworld that's been built to keep us under control. The people in its thrall are literally suspended, helpless in their servitude to a larger technological intelligence. The solution to this very real human problem is the same solution presented by Buddhism and Gnosticism—we must, like Neo, awaken.

. . . . .

It's becoming more and more obvious. I live on the edge of a Matrix-style sleep, as do we all. On one side: a bright future where we are always connected to our friends and lovers, never without an aid for reminiscence or a reminder of our social connections. On the other side: the twilight of our pre-Internet youths. And wasn't there something . . . ? Some quality . . . ?

I began this chapter lamenting little Benjamin's confusion over the difference between a touch-sensitive iPad screen and a hard copy of *Vanity Fair*. But now I have a confession to make. I'm not much better off. This is not a youth-only phenomenon. A 2013 study from the University of Michigan found that those of us in our late thirties have now reached the point of having as many electronic interactions as we have face-to-face interactions. What a dubious honor that is—to be the first generation in history to have as many exchanges with avatars as with people. I wonder, sometimes, if this means I'll start to treat friends and family as avatars in person. Occasionally, I'm hit with how weirdly *consistent* a group of people appears during a dinner party—how weird it is that they aren't changing or scrolling like thumbnail portraits

....

5. This is, yes, a hyped-up Hollywood version of Plato's "Allegory of the Cave."

on a Twitter feed, being replaced, or flicking off. I'm suffering the same brain slips that young Benjamin suffered when he tried to use a hard-copy magazine as a digital interface. The only difference is that I'm more freaked out.

Increasingly, I notice small moments when I treat hard-copy material as though it were digital. I've seen my fingers reach instinctively to zoom in to a printed photo or flick across a paper page as though to advance the progress of an e-book. These slips are deeply disturbing, a little like early signs of dementia. And they crop up in more meaningful scenarios, too. Just the other day, while discussing a particularly dreadful acquaintance with a friend of mine, I actually said, "Ugh, *unfollow*," using Twitter's term for removing an avatar from one's ranks. And it wasn't a semantic joke, is the thing. I clicked a button in my head and felt that jerk's swift removal from my mental address book.

There is one key difference here between young Benjamin and me. I am aware of my own confusion and can confront it. I can still recall my analog youth.

In the quiet suburb where I was raised, there was a green hill near our house, a place where no one ever went. It was an easy trek, over the backyard fence and up a dirt path, and I would go there on weekends with a book if I wanted to escape the company of family or merely remove myself from the stultifying order of a household. Children do need moments of solitude as well as moments of healthy interaction. (How else would they learn that the mind makes its own happiness?) But too often these moments of solitude are only stumbled upon by children, whereas socialization is constantly arranged. I remember—I was nine years old—I remember lying on the green hill and reading my book or merely staring for a long, long time at the sky. There would be a crush of childish thoughts that would eventually dissipate, piece by piece, until I was left alone with my bare consciousness, an experience that felt as close to religious rapture as I ever had. I could feel the chilled sunlight on my face and was only slightly awake to the faraway hum of traffic. This will sound more than a little fey, but that young boy on the hillside did press daisies into his book of poetry. And just the other day, when I took that book down from its dusty post on my shelf, the same pressed flowers fell out of its pages (after a quarter century of stillness) and dropped onto my bare toes. There was a deep sense memory, then, that returned me to that hushed state of mind on the lost green hill, a state that I have so rarely known since. And to think: That same year, a British computer scientist at CERN called Tim Berners-Lee was writing the code for the World Wide Web. I'm writing these words on the quarter-century anniversary of his invention.

That memory of a quieter yesteryear is dearly useful. Awake— or at least partly so—to the tremendous influence of today's tech-littered landscape, I have the choice to say yes and no to the wondrous utility of these machines, their promise and power. I do not know that Benjamin will have that same choice.

Regardless, the profound revelations of neuroplasticity re-search are constantly reinscribing the fundamental truth that we never really outgrow our environments. That the old, like the young, are vulnerable to any brave new world they find them-selves walking through. The world we fashion for ourselves, or think we fashion, remains an insistent shaper of our minds until the day we die. So, in fact, we are all Kids These Days.

Despite the universality of this change, which we're all buffeted by, there is a single, seemingly small change that I'll be most sorry about. It will sound meaningless, but: One doesn't see teenagers staring into space anymore. Gone is the idle mind of the adolescent.

I think that strange and wonderful things occur to us in those youthful time snacks, those brief reprieves when the fancy wanders. We know that many scientists and artists spring from childhoods of social deprivation. The novels of Anthony Trol-lope, for example, are the products of a friendless youth. He describes in his autobiography years and years of boyish day-dreaming, which continued in adulthood:

Other boys would not play with me. . . . Thus it came to pass that I was always going about with some castle in the air. . . . There can, I imagine, hardly be a more dangerous mental practice; but I have often doubted whether, had it not been my practice, I should ever have written a novel. I learned in this way to maintain an interest in a fictitious story, to dwell on a work created by my own imagination, and to live in a world altogether outside the world of my own material life.

Solitude may cause discomfort, but that discomfort is often a healthy and inspiring sort. It's only in moments of absence that a daydreaming person like Anthony Trollope can receive truly unexpected notions. What will become of all those surreptitious gifts when our blank spaces are filled in with duties to "social networks" and the relentless demands of our tech addictions?

I fear we are the last of the daydreamers. I fear our children will lose lack, lose absence, and never comprehend its quiet, immeasurable value. If the next generation socializes more online than in the so-called real world, and if they have no memory of a time when the reverse was true, it follows that my peers and I are the last to feel the static surrounding online socialization. The Internet becomes "the real world" and our physical reality becomes the thing that needs to be defined and set aside—"my analog life," "my snail life," "my empty life."

Montaigne once wrote, "We must reserve a back shop, all our own, entirely free, in which to establish our real liberty and our principal retreat and solitude." But where will tomorrow's children set up such a shop, when the world seems to conspire against the absentee soul?

CHAPTER 3
Confession

The highest and most beautiful things in life are not to be heard about, nor read about, nor seen but, if one will, are to be lived.

—Søren Kierkegaard

THE third most Googled person in 2012 was a small fifteen-year-old girl from Port Coquitlam—a nondescript Canadian town composed mainly of box stores, parking lots, and teenagers with nothing to do. The girl's name was Amanda Todd. She liked cheerleading—being petite, she got to be the girl at the top of the pyramid. And she liked to sing—she would perform covers before her computer's camera and post the videos on YouTube under an account titled SomeoneToKnow. In these, her adolescent pursuits, she was entirely typical. But when Amanda Todd killed herself on Wednesday, October 10, a different light was cast on her seemingly ordinary life; within days, media alighted on the most notorious cyberbullying case in history.

I will not fill these pages with a detailed account of the years of abuse that led up to her death (that story is readily available on the Internet, which proved such an entrenched and toxic commentator on Todd). Suffice it to say that when still in grade seven, she was convinced by an unidentified man to expose her breasts via webcam. That man then proceeded to blackmail and harass her with the captured image of her nude body for years. ("Put on a show for me," he would later order.) Todd became the subject of a tormenting Facebook profile, which featured her breasts as its profile picture. She attended three schools in the space of a year in an effort to avoid the ensuing harassment from peers. She was beaten by a gang of young girls (while others stood by and recorded the scene on their phones). And, eventually, Todd became so paranoid and anxious that she could not leave her home. She first attempted to kill herself by drinking from a bottle of bleach, which was unsuccessful and led to more of the online bullying that drove her to that action in the first place.

Then, a month before her death, Todd posted a video on her YouTube channel, unpacking her troubled story. This time she wasn't singing someone else's song, but describing for viewers (in a broken way, for she suffered from a language-based learning disability) her own suffering. Naturally, this opened her again to the attacks of faceless online "commenters." By stepping into the buzzing crowds of Internet forums, we hazard a deep cruelty. While Amanda Todd lived, these waves of ridicule pushed her toward more public confessions, which were broadcast over the very mass communication technologies that had spurred her distress. Later, after her suicide, she was transformed into a meme and a hashtag, bandied about online in a series of suicide jokes and vandalisms on her memorial pages. She is taunted in death even more than she was in life.

What interests me more than the common tale of online abuse, though, is the outlet that Todd turned to as a balm for her wounds—the video she posted as a final creative act. She turned, against all reason except perhaps that of an addict, to the very thing that made her suffer so. She turned to an online broadcast technology. When I first read about this tortured girl, I kept wondering how much we all subvert our emotional lives into our technologies; how much of the pain and suffering we each live with is now funneled away from traditional outlets (diaries, friends, counselors) and toward an online network that promises solace.

Two weeks after Todd killed herself, her mother, Carol, sat on a black sofa and spoke to the media. "It's not about a child who . . . just sat on her computer in her room," she said. She spoke with a soft and uncertain voice. She did not look into the camera. She tried to describe her daughter's state of mind in the days leading up to that final act. "She realized the error in her actions, but that error couldn't be erased. . . . She tried to forget, she tried to make it go away. She tried to change schools. But wherever she went, it followed her." The footage is hard to watch; Carol Todd looks understandably distraught and annoyed by the attention of the media. In the end, she bites her lip, says to the scores of imagined "bad mom" accusers, "Amanda was born into the right family." And then she asks for the camera to be turned off.

When, months later, I asked Carol Todd for an interview, she deferred or canceled our meeting a half-dozen times; her reasons sometimes seemed genuine and sometimes not. I'd resigned myself to not meeting her at all when she had an apparent change of heart and asked me to lunch. So I traveled to her hometown and sat myself down at a restaurant she likes called Earl's, where pretty, polished girls, about the age Amanda would be by now, brought us our sandwiches and coffee.

Carol Todd—in thick-rimmed glasses and a black hoodie— seemed a sedate woman, though a determined one. She was guarded when she met me, having already grown hardened by the treatment of media following her daughter's death. And she had another reason to be suspicious: In the wake of everything, she'd become a victim of cyberbullying herself. A few committed individuals from around the world send her messages, attacks on her daughter, attacks on herself. They are relentless. In several e-mails she sent me before and after our interview, she expressed her anxiety about the "haters" who were "out there."

Like her daughter, Carol responded to such harassment not by retreating, but by broadcasting herself more. She began to maintain a regular blog, where she advocates for reform in schools and governments. She set up a legacy fund to support her cause and speaks to politicians or packed gymnasiums about her experience. She has even produced a line of clothing and wrist-bands, emblazoned with her daughter's name, to raise funds. When YouTube took down Amanda's video in the days following her death, Carol requested that the video be made live again because "it was something that needed to be watched by many."

She tells me that something in the world was stirred following her daughter's death. "Amanda put herself out there. I mean, she wasn't an angel; I'm the first to admit that. But she did what she did, and I do think it woke up the world." The media outlets that picked up the story include *The New Yorker, Anderson Cooper 360°,* and *Dateline.* Vigils were held in thirty-eight countries.

"Amanda wasn't unique in having all this happen to her, though," I said. "Why did she become such a rallying force?"

"Well, it was the video, obviously. It was always the video. If she hadn't made that video, you wouldn't be sitting here."

She was right, of course. We have all, in some way, become complicit in the massive broadcasting that online life invites. But occasionally someone—usually a digital native like Amanda—will shock us awake by turning a banal thing like YouTube into a scorching confessional.

And everyone wants to hear a confession. On the evening of Todd's death, her mother looked at the video and saw it had twenty-eight hundred views. The next morning, there were ten thousand. Two weeks later, the video had been watched seventeen million times.

It was uploaded to YouTube on September 7, 2012. The picture is black and white. Todd stands before the camera, visible from just below the eyes down to her waist. She holds up, and flips through, a series of flash cards that detail her travails of the few years previous. I still remember adolescent angst and bullying as a deeply private struggle, so for me it's uncomfortable to watch her feed her trauma into a system like YouTube, to watch her give over so much of herself. The song "Hear You Me" by the band Jimmy Eat World plays softly in the background. Todd flips silently through her flash cards. The script on her cards is simple and, by adult standards, sentimental. It is also a naked cry for help that the YouTube community responded to with unavailing praise and cool scorn. The girls who physically assaulted Todd posted their own cruel comments within hours of the video's being uploaded.

· · · · ·

Extraordinary as Todd's suicide may have been, we should pause here to note that the violence of her reaction to online harassment is not an anomaly. Recent research from Michigan State University found that, for example, Singapore children who were bullied online became just as likely to consider suicide as those who were bullied offline. In fact, researchers found that cyberbullying produced slightly more suicidal thoughts: 22 percent of students who were physically bullied reported suicidal thoughts, and that number rose to 28 percent in the case of students who were bullied online.

Todd was hardly alone in all this. The stories of a heartless online world keep coming. I recently read about a University of Guelph student who decided to broadcast his suicide live online—using the notorious 4chan message board to attract an audience willing to watch him burn to death in his dorm room. (The twenty-year-old man was stopped midattempt and taken to the hospital with serious injuries.) His message to his viewers: "I thought I would finally give back to the community in the best way possible: I am willing to an hero [commit suicide][6] on cam for you all." Another 4chan user set up a video chat room for him. Two hundred watched (the chat room's limit) as he downed pills and vodka before setting his room on fire and crawling under a blanket. As the fire began to consume him, the young man appears to have typed to his viewers from beneath the covers: "#omgimonfire." Some users on the message board egged him on, suggesting more poetic ways to die. These desperate actions make for an extreme example, but I think they speak to something common in us, in fact. Most of us don't wish to give our lives over entirely to the anonymous Internet, but there is yet a disturbing intensity to the self-broadcasting that most of us have learned to adore.

To some degree, we all live out our emotional lives through technologies. We're led into deep intimacies with our gadgets precisely because our brains are imbued with a compulsion to socialize, to connect whenever possible, and connection is what our technologies are so good at offering. Some of my friends literally sleep with their phones and check their e-mail before rolling out of bed, as though the machine were a lover that demands a good-morning kiss. E-mails and tweets and blog posts might easily be dull or cruel—but the machine itself is blameless and feels like a true companion. The bond we have with our "user friendly" machines is so deep, in fact, it makes us confess things we would never confess to our suspect fellow humans.

Yet every time we use our technologies as a mediator for the chaotic elements of our lives, and every time we insist on *managing* our representation with a posted video or Facebook update, we change our relationship with those parts of our lives that we

....

6. To "an hero" is a synonym for committing suicide that is used by 4chan communities.

seek to control. We hold some part of the world at a distance, and since we are forever *of* the world, we end up holding some part of ourselves at a distance, too. The repercussions of this alienation can be trivial—I've heard from many young girls worried about whether some schoolmate has "friended" them or "followed" them—but they can also be deeply, irrevocably tragic.

Perhaps we shouldn't be surprised when digital natives look for comfort in the very media that torments them. What else would they know to do? As Evgeny Morozov points out in *The Net Delusion*, if the only hammer you are given is the Internet, "it's not surprising that every possible social and political problem is presented as an online nail." Morozov expanded on that analogy in his more recent *To Save Everything, Click Here,* where he wrote: "It's a very powerful set of hammers, and plenty of people—many of them in Silicon Valley—are dying to hear you cry, 'Nail!' regardless of what you are looking at." It's easy, in other words, to become convinced that the solution to a tech-derived problem is more technology. Particularly when that technology has enveloped our entire field of vision. While someone of my generation might see that the Internet is not the entire toolbox, for Todd and her cohort, unplugging the problem—or at least the problem's mouthpiece—isn't an apparent option.

Without memories of an unplugged world, the subversion of human emotion to online management systems seems like the finest, most expedient, and certainly easiest way to deal.

Ultimately, we desire machines that can understand our feelings perfectly and even supervise our feelings for us.

There's an entrenched irony, though, in our relationships with "social" media. They obliterate distance, yet make us lonely. They keep us "in touch," yet foster an anxiety around physical interaction. As MIT's Sherry Turkle put it so succinctly: "We bend to the inanimate with new solicitude." In her interviews with youths about their use of technologies versus interactions with warm human bodies, the young regularly pronounce other people "risky" and technologies "safe." Here is one of her more revealing interview subjects, Howard, discussing the potential for a robotic guardian:

> There are things, which you cannot tell your friends or your parents, which . . . you could tell an AI [artificial intelligence]. Then it would give you advice you could be more sure of. . . . I'm assuming it would be programmed with prior knowledge of situations and how they worked out. Knowledge of you, probably knowledge of your friends, so it could make a reasonable decision for your course of action. I know a lot of teenagers, in particular, tend to be caught up in emotional things and make some really bad mistakes because of that.

As yet, no such robot is ready for Howard.

· · · · ·

The quasi-biblical quest to bequeath unto computers an emotional intelligence—to "promote them" from darkness—has long occupied human imagination and appears to have proceeded down a pair of intertwining roads. Down one road, typified by Mary Shelley's *Frankenstein,* the birth of artificial intelligence has harrowing repercussions, however soulful its beginnings. Down the other road, we encounter the robot as savior or selfless aide, as seen in Leonardo da Vinci's 1495 designs for a mechanical knight. Mostly, though, these two roads have crossed over each other—the artificial being is both savior and villain. As Adam and Eve were corrupted and disappointed their God, so our science-fiction writers presume robot intelligence will start off with noble intentions and lead to an inevitable debasement. This twinned identity of friend and antagonist is evident as far back as 1921, when the Czech dramatist Karel Čapek premiered his play *R.U.R.* The acronym stands for *Rossum's Universal Robots* (this was in fact the work that popularized the term *robot*). In Čapek's play, a line of helpful mechanical servants degrades into hostile rebels that attack their human masters and eventually kill us off.

Shelves and shelves of such dystopian fantasies do not dull, though, the hope that our creations may know something we do not, may ease our human suffering. We turn to that promise of artificial intelligence almost with the instincts of lost children, asking them to make sense of our lives or help us to escape the silence of our solitude. It makes sense, then, that the first computer outside of science fiction to speak back with something akin to human concern was an infinitely patient and infinitely permissive therapist called ELIZA.

In the mid-1960s, Joseph Weizenbaum, a computer scientist at MIT, wrote a string of code that allowed a computer to process conversational text and then produce a new piece of text that looked an awful lot like the next step in a dialogue. ELIZA was named for Eliza Doolittle, the Cockney girl in George Bernard Shaw's play *Pygmalion,* who must overcome her impoverished upbringing and learn to speak "like a lady." The program's efforts to communicate were rudimentary, and her speech was annoyingly reflective in the manner of a Rogerian psychologist. Tell ELIZA, "I don't like going to school," and she will respond with, "Tell me why you don't like going to school." Inform ELIZA that the room is dark, and she will ask if you really think that is so.

I was able to use the ELIZA program myself, thinking it could do a better job of explaining its workings than I could. Here is the transcript from our first session:

Hello. My name is Eliza. How may I help you?

I want to write about you.

Oh . . . ?

Yes, I'm writing a book and there's a chapter where you appear.

How long have you been writing a book and there's a chapter where me appear?

A few months now.

I'm not sure I understand you fully.

I'm not sure you do, either.

Do you believe it is normal to be not sure me does either?

I think it's probably a typical response to your responses.

Why are you concerned about my responses?

Mainly because they're nonsensical.

That is quite interesting.

Do you think so?

You're not really talking about me, are you?

This quickly grew insufferable. But perhaps, I told myself, the experiment was unfair. Self-reflection is not what ELIZA was designed to excel at. She wanted to help me with my problems, not discuss her own secrets. I tried again, this time with a genuine emotional approach.

Hello. My name is Eliza. How may I help you?

I'm stressed about writing a book.

How long have you been stressed about writing a book?

Months.

Okay. . . . "I'm stressed about writing a book." Tell me more.

Like what?

Does that question interest you?

Oh, fuck off.

Tell me more. . . .

Fuck off. Fuck off. Fuck off.

Why do you repeat yourself?

Fuck off. Fuck off. Fuck off.

Come, come, elucidate your thoughts.

Fuck, fuck, fuckity fuck.

Say, do you have any psychological problems?

This second attempt at communicating with the antique program counted as a failure, too, I think. But I *was* surprised at
how engaged I felt.

When Weizenbaum began allowing MIT students to interact
with ELIZA, he, too, was surprised by how drawn in they were.
Many of them found her approach charming and helpful. She
was, in some ways, an ideal conversationalist: someone willing
to parrot back your own opinions and ask over and over how
you feel and why you feel that way. Some therapists (hardly looking out for their own financial interests) began suggesting that
ELIZA would be a cheap alternative to pricey psychoanalysis
sessions. As dull-witted as ELIZA actually was, she gave people
exactly what they wanted from a listener—a sounding board.
"Extremely short exposures to a relatively simple computer program," Weizenbaum later wrote, "could induce powerful delu-
sional thinking in quite normal people."

Today, these delusions are everywhere. Often they manifest
in ridiculous ways. BMW was forced to recall a GPS system because German men couldn't take directions from the computer's
female voice. And when the U.S. Army designed its Sergeant Star,
a chatbot that talks to would-be recruits at GoArmy.com, they

naturally had their algorithm speak with a burly, all-American voice reminiscent of the shoot-'em-up video game *Call of Duty*. Fooling a human into bonding with inanimate programs (often of corporate or governmental derivation) is the new, promising, and dangerous frontier. But the Columbus of that frontier set sail more than half a century ago.

· · · · ·

The haunted English mathematician Alan Turing—godfather of the computer—believed that a future with emotional, companionable computers was a simple inevitability. He declared, "One day ladies will take their computers for walks in the park and tell each other, 'My little computer said such a funny thing this morning!' " Turing proposed that a machine could be called "intelligent" if people exchanging text messages with that machine could not tell whether they were communicating with a human. (There are a few people I know who would fail such a test, but that is another matter.)

This challenge—which came to be called "the Turing test"— lives on in an annual competition for the Loebner Prize, a coveted solid-gold medal (plus $100,000 cash) for any computer whose conversation is so fluid, so believable, that it becomes indistinguishable from a human correspondent.[7] At the Loebner competition (founded in 1990 by New York philanthropist Hugh Loebner), a panel of judges sits before computer screens and engages in brief, typed conversations with humans and computers— but they aren't told which is which. Then the judges must cast their votes—which was the person and which was the program? Programs like Cleverbot (the "most human computer" in 2005 and 2006) maintain an enormous database of typical responses

....

7. The gold medal has not been won yet. Smaller prizes are given each year for the "most human computer" in the bunch.

that humans make to given sentences, which they cobble together into legible (though slightly bizarre) conversations; others, like the 2012 winner, Chip Vivant, eschew the database of canned responses and attempt something that passes for "reasoning." Human contestants are liable to be deemed inhuman, too: One warm-blooded contestant called Cynthia Clay, who happened to be a Shakespeare expert, was voted a computer by three judges when she started chatting about the Bard and seemed to know "too much." (According to Brian Christian's account in *The Most Human Human*, Clay took the mistake as a badge of honor—being inhuman was a kind of compliment.)

All computer contestants, like ELIZA, have failed the full Turing test; the infinitely delicate set of variables that makes up human exchange remains opaque and uncomputable. Put simply, computers still lack the empathy required to meet humans on their own emotive level.

We inch toward that goal. But there is a deep difficulty in teaching our computers even a little empathy. Our emotional expressions are vastly complex and incorporate an annoyingly subtle range of signifiers. A face you read as tired may have all the lines and shadows of "sorrowful" as far as a poorly trained robot is concerned.

What Alan Turing imagined, an intelligent computer that can play the human game at least almost as well as a real human, is now called "affective computing"—and it's the focus of a burgeoning field in computer science. "Affective" is a curious word choice, though an apt one. While the word calls up "affection" and has come to reference moods and feelings, we should remember that "affective" comes from the Latin word *afficere*, which means "to influence" or (more sinisterly) "to attack with disease."

Recently, a band of scientists at MIT has made strides toward the holy grail of *afficere*—translating the range of human emotions into the 1s and 0s of computer code.

· · · · ·

Besides the progress of chatbots, we now have software that can map twenty-four points on your face, allowing it to identify a range of emotions and issue appropriate responses. We also have Q sensors—bands worn on the wrist that measure your "emotional arousal" by monitoring body heat and the skin's electrical conductance.

But the root problem remains unchanged. Whether we're talking about "affective computers" or "computational empathy," at a basic level we're still discussing pattern recognition technology and the ever more sophisticated terrain of data mining. Always, the goal is to "humanize" an interface by the enormous task of filtering masses of lived experience through a finer and finer mesh of software.

Many of the minds operating at the frontier of this effort come together at MIT's Media Lab, where researchers are busy (in their own words) "inventing a better future." I got to know Karthik Dinakar, a Media Lab researcher who moonlights with Microsoft, helping them improve their Bing search engine. ("Every time you type in 'Hillary Clinton,'" he told me, "that's me.")

Dinakar is a handsome twenty-eight-year-old man with tight black hair and a ready smile. And, like Amanda Todd, he's intimately acquainted with the harshness of childhood bullying. Dinakar was bullied throughout his teen years for being "too geeky," and he would reach out online. "I would write blog posts and I would . . . well, I would feel lighter. I think that's why people do all of it, why they go on Twitter or anywhere. I think they must be doing it for sympathy of one kind or another."

Compounding Dinakar's sense of difference was the fact that he lives with an extreme variety of synesthesia; this means his brain creates unusual sensory impressions based on seemingly unrelated inputs. We've all experienced synesthesia to some degree: The brain development of infants actually necessitates a similar state of being. Infants at two or three months still have intermingled senses. But in rare cases, the situation will persist. If you mention the number "seven" to Dinakar, he sees a distinct color. "Friday" is always a particular dark green. "Sunday" is always black.

Naturally, these differences make Dinakar an ideal member of the Media Lab team. A so-called geek with a brain hardwired to make unorthodox connections is exactly what a bastion of interdisciplinary academia most desperately needs.

When Dinakar began his PhD work at MIT, in the fall of 2010, his brain was "in pain for the entire semester," he says. Class members were told to come up with a single large project, but nothing came to mind. "I wasn't interested in what others were interested in. There was just . . . nothing. I assumed I was going to flunk."

Then, one evening at home, Dinakar watched Anderson Cooper report on Tyler Clementi, an eighteen-year-old violin student at Rutgers University who had leapt from the George Washington Bridge and drowned in the Hudson River. Clementi's dorm mate had encouraged friends to watch him kissing another boy via a secretly positioned webcam. The ubiquitous Dr. Phil appeared on the program, speaking with Cooper about the particular lasting power of cyberbullying, which does not disappear the way a moment of "real-life bullying" might: "This person thinks, 'I am damaged, irreparably, forever.' And that's the kind of desperation that leads to an act of suicide. . . . The thought of the victim is that everybody in the world has seen this. And that everybody in the world is going to respond to it like the mean-spirited person that created it." Dinakar watched the program, figuring there must be a way to stem such cruelty, to monitor and manage unacceptable online behavior.

Most social Web sites leave it to the public. Facebook, Twitter, and the like incorporate a button that allows users to "flag this as inappropriate" when they see something they disapprove of. In the age of crowdsourced knowledge like Wikipedia's, such user-driven moderation sounds like common sense, and perhaps it is.[8] "But what happens," Dinakar explains, "is that all flagging goes into a stream where a moderation team has to look at it. Nobody gets banned automatically, so the problem becomes how do you deal with eight hundred million users throwing up content and flagging each other?" (Indeed, Facebook has well over one billion users whose actions it must manage.) "The truth is that the moderation teams are so shockingly small compared with the amount of content they must moderate that there's simply no way it can be workable. What I realized was that technology must help the moderators. I found that, strangely, nobody was working on this."

The most rudimentary algorithms, when searching for abusive behavior online, can spot a word like "faggot" or "slut" but remain incapable of contextualizing those words. For example, such an algorithm would flag this paragraph as bully material simply because those words appear in it. Our brains and our meaning, however, do not work in an "on" and "off" way. The attainment of meaning requires a subtle understanding of context, which is something computers have trouble with. What Dinakar wanted to deliver was a way to identify abusive *themes.* "The brain," he told me, "is multinominal." We think, in other words, by combining several terms in relation to one another, not merely by identifying particular words. "If I tell a guy he'd look good in lipstick," says Dinakar, "a computer would not pick that up as a potential form of abuse. But a human knows that this could be a kind of bullying." Now Dinakar just had to teach a computer to do the same.

The solution came in the form of latent Dirichlet allocation (LDA), a complex language-processing model derived in 2003 that can discover topics from within the mess of infinite arrangements of words the human brain spews forth. LDA is multinominal, like

....

8. Such content will almost definitely be managed more tightly in the future than it is now—perhaps by the government. To paraphrase Microsoft researcher danah boyd: Facebook is a utility; utilities get regulated.

our brains, and works with what Dinakar calls "that bag-of-associations thing." Dinakar began with a simple assumption about the bag of associations he was looking for: "If we try to detect power differentials between people, we can begin to weed out cases of bullying."

The work was barely under way when Dinakar received a letter from the Executive Office of the President of the United States. Would he like to come to a summit in D.C.? Yes, he said.

There he met Aneesh Chopra—the inaugural chief technology officer of the United States—who was chairing the panel on cyberbullying that Dinakar had been invited to join. Three years later, Dinakar has the White House's backing on a new project he's calling the National Helpline, a combined governmental and NGO effort that means to, for the first time, begin dealing with the billions of desperate messages in bottles that teens are throwing online. The National Helpline incorporates artificial intelligence to analyze problems that are texted in, then produces resources and advice specific to each problem. It is one of the most humane nonhuman systems yet constructed. The effort is fueled in part by Dinakar's frustration with the limits of traditional psychiatry, which is "mostly based on single-subject studies and is often very retrospective. They come up with all these umbrella terms that are very loosely defined. And there's no data anywhere. There is no data *anywhere*. I think it's a very peculiar field."

By contrast, Dinakar's National Helpline—in addition to providing its automated and tailored advice—will amass an enormous amount of data, which will be stored and analyzed in a kind of e–health bank. "We'll be analyzing every instance with such granularity," says Dinakar. "And hopefully this will help psychiatry to become a much more hard science. Think about it. This is such an unexplored area. . . . We can mine photos of depressed people and get information on depression in a way that no one at any other point in history could have done."

The reduction of our personal lives to mere data does run the risk of collapsing things into a Big Brother scenario, with algorithms like Dinakar's scouring the Internet for "unfriendly" behavior and dishing out "correction" in one form or another.[9]

One Carnegie Mellon researcher, Alessandro Acquisti, has shown that in some cases facial recognition software can analyze a photo and within thirty seconds deliver that person's Social Security number. Combine this with algorithms like Dinakar's and perhaps I could ascertain a person's emotional issues after snapping his or her photo on the street. The privacy issues that plague our online confessions are something Dinakar is aware of, but he leaves policy to the policy makers. "I don't have an answer about that," he told me. "I guess it all depends on how we use this technology. But I don't have an answer as to how that should be."[10] I don't think any of us do, really. In our rush toward confession and connection—all those happy status updates and geo-tagged photo uploads—rarely do we consider how thorough a "confession" we're really making. Nor do we consider to what authority we're doing the confessing. This is because the means of confession—the technology itself—is so very amiable. Dinakar is building a more welcoming online world, and it's a good thing he is. But we need to remain critical as we give over so much of ourselves to algorithmic management.

....

9. Governments and corporations may use such programs to keep tabs on the whereabouts of "unfriendly" persons. For example, *The Guardian* reported on February 10, 2013, that "defense giant Raytheon has created software capable of tracking people based on information posted to social networks. Its capabilities are impressively creepy." Raytheon's software, called Riot, extracts location information from Facebook or the location tags on uploaded photos, joining a long list of technologies that make mass surveillance (of "terrorists" and "innocents" alike) more feasible.

10. Mostly, Dinakar's vision is a cheerful, hopeful one. I ask him how he imagines the future, and he begins to describe the talking paintings that J. K. Rowling included in her Harry Potter books. "Thirty or fifty years from now," he says, "the paintings will talk to you. If I have a picture of my mom, who lives back in India, and she's happy, then the picture in my home will look happy. I will know how she feels in the moment she feels it."

· · · · ·

In a sense, Dinakar and others at the Media Lab are still pursuing Alan Turing's dream. "I want to compute for empathy," Dinakar told me as our time together wound down. "I don't want to compute for banning anyone. I just want . . . I want the world to be a less lonely place." Of course, for such affective computing to work the way its designers intend, we must be prepared to give ourselves over to its care.

How far would such handling by algorithms go? How cared for shall we be? "I myself can sometimes think in a very reactive way," says Dinakar. He imagines that, one day, technologies like the software he's working on could help us manage all kinds of baser instincts. "I'd like it if my computer read my e-mail and told me about the consequences when I hit a Send button. I would like a computer that would tell me to take five deep breaths. A technology that could make me more self-aware."

A part of me has a knee-jerk reaction against the management Dinakar is describing. Do we want to abstract, monitor, quantify, ourselves so?

Then I think again about the case of Amanda Todd and whether such online watchdogs might have helped her. Only one in six suicides is accompanied by an actual suicide note, but it's estimated that three-quarters of suicide attempts are preceded by some warning signs—signs we hapless humans fail to act on. Sometimes the signs are explicit: Tyler Clementi updated his Facebook page to read, "Jumping off the GW Bridge sorry." Sometimes the messages are more obscure: Amanda Todd's video merely suggests deep depression. How much can be done when those warning signs are issued in the empathic vacuum of the Internet? Are we not obliged to try to humanize that which processes so much of our humanity? Dinakar's software could help those who reach out directly to it— but here's the rub: When we go online, we commit ourselves to the care of online mechanisms. Digital Band-Aids for digital wounds.

We feed ourselves into machines, hoping some algorithm will digest the mess that is our experience into something legible, something more meaningful than the "bag of associations" we fear we are. Nor do the details of our lives need to be drawn from us by force. We do all the work ourselves.

We all of us love to broadcast, to call ourselves into existence against the obliterating silence that would otherwise dominate so much of our lives. Perhaps teenage girls offer the ultimate example, projecting their avatars insistently into social media landscapes with an army of selfies, those ubiquitous self-portraits taken from a phone held at arm's length; the pose—often pouting—is a mainstay of Facebook (one that sociologist Ben Agger has called "the male gaze gone viral"). But as Nora Young points out in her book *The Virtual Self,* fervent self-documentation extends far beyond the problematic vanities of teenage girls. Some of us wear devices that track our movements and sleep patterns, then post results on Web sites devoted to constant comparison; others share their sexual encounters and exercise patterns; we "check in" to locations using GPS-enabled services like Foursquare.com; we publish our minute-by-minute musings, post images of our meals and cocktails before consuming them, as devotedly as others say grace. Today, when we attend to our technologies, we *elect* to divulge information, free of charge and all day long. We sing our songs to the descendants of Alan Turing's machines, now designed to consume not merely neutral computations, but the triumphs, tragedies, and minutiae of lived experience—we deliver children opening their Christmas presents; middle-aged men ranting from their La-Z-Boys; lavishly choreographed wedding proposals.

There's a basic pleasure in accounting for a life that, in reality, is always somewhat inchoate. Young discusses the "gold star" aspect of that moment when we broadcast ourselves: "Self-tracking is . . . revelatory, and consequently, for some of us at least, motivating." In reality, life outside of orderly institutions like schools, jobs, and prisons is lacking in "gold star" moments; it passes by in a not-so-dignified way, and nobody tells us whether we're getting it right or wrong. But publish your experience online and an institutional approval system rises to meet it—your photo is "liked," your status is gilded with commentary. It's even a way to gain some sense of immortality, since online publishing creates a lasting record, a living scrapbook. This furthers our enjoyable sense of an ordered life. We become consistent, we are approved, we are a known and sanctioned quantity.

If a good life, today, is a recorded life, then a great life is a famous one. Yalda T. Uhls, a researcher at UCLA's Children's Digital Media Center, delivered a conference presentation in the spring of 2013 called "Look at ME," in which she analyzed the most popular TV shows for tween audiences from 1967 to 2007. The post-Internet television content (typified by *American Idol* and *Hannah Montana*) had swerved dramatically from family-oriented shows like *Happy Days* in previous decades. "Community feeling" had been a dominant theme in content from 1967 to 1997; then, in the final decade leading up to 2007, fame became an overwhelming focus (it was one of the least important values in tween television in earlier years). Uhls points out that the most significant environmental change in that final decade was the advent of the Internet and, more to the point, platforms such as YouTube and Facebook, which "encourage broadcasting yourself and sharing aspects of your life to people beyond your face-to-face community. . . . In other words, becoming famous."[11] One recent survey of three thousand British parents confirmed this position when it found that the top three job aspirations of children today are sportsman, pop star, and actor. Twenty-five years ago, the top three aspirations were teacher, banker, and doctor.

....

11. Uhls's research indicates that there is, not surprisingly, a relationship between valuing fame and usage of social media.

If the glory of fame has indeed trumped humbler ambitions, then the ethos of YouTube is an ideal medium for the message. Its tantalizing tagline: "Broadcast Yourself."

. . . . .

We feel a strange duality when watching a YouTube video like Amanda Todd's. The video is at once deeply private and unabashedly public. This duality seems familiar, though: The classic handwritten diary, secured perhaps with a feeble lock and key, shoved to the bottom of the underwear drawer, suggests an abhorrence of the casual, uninvited reader; but isn't there also a secret hope that those confessions will be read by an idealized interloper? We desire both protection and revelation for our soul's utterance. W. H. Auden wrote, "The image of myself which I try to create in my own mind in order that I may love myself is very different from the image which I try to create in the minds of others in order that they may love me." But broadcast videos like Amanda Todd's attempt to collapse those two categories. Bending both inward and outward, they confuse the stylized public persona and the raw private confession.

What, then, is the material difference between making our confessions online, to the bewildering crowds of comment makers, and making our confessions in the calm and private cloister of a paper diary? What absence have we lost?

When we make our confessions online, we abandon the powerful workshop of the lone mind, where we puzzle through the mysteries of our own existence without reference to the demands of an often ruthless public.

Our ideas wilt when exposed to scrutiny too early—and that includes our ideas about ourselves. But we almost never remember that. I know that in my own life, and in the lives of my friends, it often seems natural, now, to reach for a broadcasting tool when anything momentous wells up. The first time I climbed the height of the Eiffel Tower I was alone, and when at last I reached the summit and looked out during a sunset at that bronzed and ancient city, my first instinct was not to take in the glory of it all, but to turn to someone next to me and say, "Isn't it awesome?" But I had come alone. So I texted my boyfriend, long distance, because the experience wouldn't be real until I had shared it, confessed my "status."

Young concludes *The Virtual Self* by asking us to recall that much of life is not "trackable," that we must be open to "that which cannot be articulated in an objective manner or reduced to statistics." It's a caution worth heeding. The idea that technology must always be a way of opening up the world to us, of making our lives richer and never poorer, is a catastrophic one. But the most insidious aspect of this trap is the way online technologies encourage confession while simultaneously alienating the confessor. I wish, for example, I had just looked out at Paris and left it at that. When I gave in to "sharing" the experience, I fumbled and dropped the unaccountable joy that life was offering up. Looking back, I think it seems obvious that efficient communication is not the ultimate goal of human experience.

Yet everywhere we seem convinced that falling trees do not make sounds unless someone (other than ourselves) can hear them. There was that one friend of mine who announced his mother's cancer diagnosis on his Facebook wall, which shocked me and seemed utterly natural to others. There was another friend who posted online the story of his boyfriend dying of AIDS (he had refused to take his meds). It's easy to say this is just about "shifting baselines." But adopting a culture of public confession is more than that: It marks the devaluing of that solitary gift— reverie.

. . . . .

When my lunch with Carol Todd was over, she fished a few pink silicon bracelets from her purse, each emblazoned with "Amanda Todd Legacy." I said, "Thanks," not sure if that's what you say.

"Will you let me see this piece before you send it to your editor?"

"Oh, we usually don't—" But she stopped me.

"You understand, I'm still her mother. I still need to protect her."

This shocked me a little, because Amanda Todd's story is now so far beyond the grip of her mother's care. There are hundreds of Web pages, there's an ocean of commentary. Yet this does nothing to assuage her maternal instinct.

As for the daughter who launched those public confessions, I believe she was standing in available light; I believe she was a hurting but blameless person, working with the tools she was given. So are we all. We each struggle through the mesh of communication technologies we inherit—to be heard, to be cared for. And we each forget, every day, how much care we need to take when using our seemingly benign tools; they are so useful and so sharp.

CHAPTER 4
Public Opinion

We all do no end of feeling and we mistake it for thinking. And out of it we get an aggregation which we consider a boon. Its name is Public Opinion.

—Mark Twain

FOR a number of years, the inventor of the hair iron was a woman named Erica Feldman. The world's arbiter of truth, Wikipedia, said so, anyway, and that was good enough for most of us. The assertion proliferated across the Internet and, to this day, remains a truth published by a number of Web sites and even, apparently, one printed book. Unfortunately, Feldman (though she may well be a real person) did not invent the hair iron, and on September 15, 2009, Wikipedia was forced to consign the Feldman affair to their growing list of hoaxes. Not a particularly scandalous or even *interesting* hoax, but such is the banality of error.

Four years later, I asked Wiki.Answers.com (the largest Q&A site online) who Erica Feldman is and was redirected to a set of crowdsourced "Relevant Answers" that claimed she is both alive and that she invented the hair straightener in 1872 (making her more than 140 years old). I was also informed of the Feldman hairdo, which involves "slicked-back long hair with one strand hanging over the forehead." These results were displayed alongside a number of hair-focused advertisements. Even the algorithms that choose which companies should hawk things at me when I search for "Erica Feldman" are in on the mass delusion.

For all its good—and nobody would deny its enormous usefulness—the "encyclopedia that anyone can edit" (as Wikipedia calls itself) has produced, in its spree of democratic knowledge production, some doozies. Once, the Web site asserted that the English composer Ronnie Hazlehurst penned a hit for the pop group S Club 7 (he emphatically did not). The information sat on Wikipedia for only ten days, yet it led to several news professionals repeating the "fact" in obituaries following Hazlehurst's death. Those news outlets, of course, could then be cited in turn, so that even people who understand that Wikipedia is only a tertiary source can, in effect, become a carrier of Wiki-untruths when they cite a supposedly reputable source. (Wikipedia itself could, arguably, proceed to cite the sources that once cited *it*, in a circular appeasement of the original lie.)

Wikipedia has broadcast information about a princess of Sigave called Tuatafa Hori; details on the great battle of Exahameron; information on *Sailor Toadstool* (a crossover between *Sailor Moon* and *Super Mario Bros.*); and many other people and things that never existed, except in the trusting confines of its own pages. The longest-known hoax of this sort is the person of Gaius Flavius Antonius, who for more than eight years was the real assassin of Julius Caesar. There are even hoaxes about hoaxes: For more than a month in the spring of 2008, one page on the Web site claimed that Margaret Thatcher was a fictitious character.

All this is hardly surprising given the Web site's prodigious output (I see there are currently about thirty-two million pages in the English Wikipedia alone). Although it's impressive to think of the thirty-two thick volumes that made up the final print version of *Encyclopædia Britannica* (released in 2010), that's a minuscule amount of content compared with Wikipedia's efforts. Printing Wikipedia in a book form similar to the *Britannica* (and without images) would necessitate about two thousand volumes. Online or in print, one simply can't create that much content without allowing for a margin of error.

And a downgrading of authority. When Clifton Fadiman, a midcentury literary lion and member of *Encyclopædia Britannica*'s board of editors, realized in the 1990s that the Internet would outdo *Britannica*, the octogenarian said, "I guess we will just have to accept the fact that minds less educated than our own will soon be in charge." Fadiman was, in his elitist way, making the same point T. S. Eliot made in 1934 when he wrote, "Where is the knowledge we have lost in information?" Where is the signal amid this noise? In a remarkably short period of time, we've moved from the eighteenth century's "Republic of Letters"—a self-selected group of intellectuals talking among themselves and generally ignoring the masses—to what we might call a "Crowd of Letters" today.

I don't know whether Fadiman was overreacting (or how we might test his assertion), but as beleaguered newspapers (and the rest of us) turn increasingly to Wikipedia as a fact-checking source, it's worth wondering how an encyclopedia devoid of traditional authority structures goes about ascertaining that slippery thing we end up calling "truth." Human error is hardly the main problem; even the revered *Britannica* is not free of mistakes. The real trouble with Wikipedia lies exactly where its strength lies: its democratic impulse. In an arena where everyone's version of the facts is equally valid, and the opinions of specialists become marginalized, corporate and politicized interests are potentially empowered.

. . . . .

James Heilman—a tall, bespectacled man, casual and jokey—believes in the Wikipedia mission. He works forty hours a week as a doctor in his small-town hospital's emergency room, then puts in a further forty hours of unpaid work for Wikipedia, editing and beefing up medical pages in his spare time. Heilman is one of the Web site's roughly eight hundred active administrators, all working in different locations around the globe and all without pay. He is deeply committed to the task: Recently, he oversaw five months of discussion about whether the lead image for the "Pregnancy" page should show a naked woman or a clothed one. (After one hundred users voted, the final decision was uploaded: clothed it is.)

Being an administrator is hardly a glorious position. When the title is conferred—after a "Request for Adminship" and a weeklong peer-review process similar to a thesis defense—the badge Wikipedia sticks on your user profile is an image of a janitor's mop and bucket, highlighting the fact that an administrator is merely a servant to the greater mission. The administrator cannot arbitrate truth, he or she can only mop toward it.

A few years back, though, Heilman became mired in a battle over the truth of Transcendental Meditation. A peer of Heilman's had asked him to check out some of the material appearing on the TM organization's page, and he found that Wikipedia was on the record stating that Transcendental Meditation had significant health benefits. Heilman reviewed the literature, found zero evidence backing up that claim, and deleted the offending text from the page.

The information quickly reappeared. While Heilman considers TM a new religion, the TM folk consider themselves scientists. The sources they began citing on "their" Wikipedia page were all studies associated with the Transcendental Meditation program.

Disputes on Wikipedia are settled by popular vote. After a fixed number of tug-of-war revisions between two parties, such votes are simply part of the process. In Heilman vs. TM, though, not enough general editors (that is, users) were interested in voting; a team of editors working with TM (a mere ten or so) was enough to win any vote over wording that came up. They had screen names like TimidGuy and LittleOlive, chosen specifically (argues Heilman) to portray an underdog.

"They are, in fact, always super-supernice people," Heilman told me. "They never exhibit frustration, they always play by the rules. They're just these nice, conscientious editors that gently, quietly, pushed their point of view onto the page over the course of years. Like all religions, they're patient and have a very good understanding of psychology."

Heilman continued to fight for his own version of the truth, one aligned with the traditional scientific method, and ended up looking for a dodge around Wikipedia's voting system. Although the vast majority of Wikipedia disputes are settled by popular vote, there is one group that could be called a higher authority: the Arbitration Committee. Two years after founding the Web site, Jimmy Wales invented the committee—he chose a dozen people (there are now fifteen)—to settle intractable disputes among editors. Heilman brought his Transcendental Meditation case before this court of last resort on two occasions.

To no effect. "The Arbitration Committee," explains Heilman, "only judges behavioral issues, not factual issues." Play nice, in other words, and your version of the truth might survive the scrutiny of someone wielding pesky facts.

I found this hard to believe, so I tracked down a member of the committee in question. Dave Craven, a thirty-two-year-old IT developer living in the northwest United Kingdom, confirmed Heilman's assertions. The process, Craven told me, is long-winded and "very bureaucratic," but, ultimately, "it's certainly the intent of the committee to deal with user conduct issues, not content issues. . . . The philosophy is quite simply our own fallibility as humans—we're just over a dozen individuals, and so we're unlikely to have the qualifications required to make judgments on every contentious issue from medicine to religion and beyond. What we *can* handle is how people are acting." Fewer and fewer cases, strangely, are brought before the Arbitration Committee. In 2006, there were 116 cases, and that number has been dropping steeply ever since. In 2013, only 12 cases were handled by the committee.

The Arbitration Committee is clearly well-meaning and serves its purpose, but Wikipedia's production of knowledge will always be influenced by insistent partiality from some corner or other—the democratic impulse seems at least as flawed as the elitist. "This is the weakness of Wikipedia," says Heilman. "With endless patience, a group can substantially alter what knowledge is presented to the world." To this day, Heilman is displeased with the Transcendental Meditation page's stance. In the end, he says, "they simply wore us down. I had to give up."

Depth, time, patience. These are where the real fault lines of Wikipedia appear. The soft, persistent, and insistent nudging of truth from one reality to another. As this grand, tertiary source is more and more unabashedly employed in the production of knowledge, it's not the blatant hoaxes or benign errors we'll need to worry about; nor are profane vandalisms a problem—they're easily spotted and deleted by computer systems designed to "reduce the burden on human beings." No, what we'll need to worry about are the interests of forces that outlive the efforts of single humans like James Heilman. Coca-Cola has all the time in the world. So does every church (with the exception of those promoting doomsday philosophies). If we can see the problem in a scenario like Heilman's battle with Transcendental Meditation, which played out over just a few years and only a decade after Wikipedia's invention, then what imperceptible changes might be wrought by such a system over centuries? (Disinformation—active deception—is far more damaging than simple errors.) What uncatchable, unnoticeable changes to human understanding would our collective, incorporated biases visit upon future generations?

And one final bias to worry about is, of course, the gender bias. The "consensus" that Wikipedia arrives at turns out to actually be a *male* consensus. In the company's own 2011 survey, a stunning 91 percent of Wikipedia editors were found to be men. The limits such gender biases create may be very severe. So the idea of pursuing truth as mass agreement still raises the question—whose mass?

· · · · ·

After our talk at a YVR bar, I watch Heilman hurry off to catch his plane, and my thoughts return to Erica Feldman and her erroneous honor.

Who, then, *did* invent the hair iron? Whose throne had "Erica Feldman" usurped? The site Wikipediocracy, which calls itself "a critical review site examining Wikipedia's flaws and follies," takes a raised-eyebrow glee in shining "the light of scrutiny into the dark crevices of Wikipedia and its related projects; to examine the corruption there, along with the structural flaws." I discovered on Wikipediocracy that "the actual inventor" of the hair iron was Madam C. J. Walker. Several other sites confirm the assertion.

Who? Walker, it turns out, was very much a real person. Born Sarah Breedlove in Louisiana, shortly before the Christmas of 1867, she was the daughter of two ex-slaves but grew up to be one of the great business leaders and philanthropists of her time. Walker spent her early life working as a laundress and then, determined to make something of herself, devised a hair care system specifically for black women. "Madam Walker's Wonderful Hair Grower" was sold by "hair culturists" trained in her own "Walker Schools." The empire expanded to the point where her payroll reportedly exceeded $200,000 per year. She died in New York in the spring of 1919, a very rich woman.

Sadly, and perhaps inevitably, further research revealed that the assertion that she invented the hair iron was another untruth. For now, at least.

In our rush to employ a world's worth of eager amateurs—and build an encyclopedia with entries about school massacres while they're still playing on the news—isn't it possible we're missing something, some pause or just a kind of breath that leads to wisdom? What was that admonishment from the poet Rainer Maria Rilke? "Live the questions now. Perhaps you will then gradually, without noticing it, live along some distant day into the answer." But we never do find time for a *lack* of knowledge. We want to know *now*. Living a question requires a fondness for absence that appears to be in short supply.

· · · · ·

When we grip our phones and tablets, we're holding the kind of information resource that governments would have killed for just a generation ago. And is it that experience of everyday information miracles, perhaps, that makes us all feel as though our own opinions are so worth sharing? After all, aren't we—in an abstracted sense, at least—just as smart as everyone else in the room, as long as we're sharing the same Wi-Fi connection? And therefore (goes the bullish leap in thinking) aren't my opinions just as worthy of trumpeting?

· · · · ·

Traditionally, expertise was a one-way road. A book might upset or even outrage a reader, but the most anyone could do was scrawl a feeble, "Not True!!!" in the margins of its pages. I've done it myself and felt the sense of impotence such ejaculations produce. What's important there is the brevity of the response. Amateurs may well have had some clever ideas that discounted the book in their lap, but they wouldn't bother to write them out because, alas, no one would read them (least of all the author, happily oblivious and working on his or her next, equally galling book). Today, however, that same author cannot escape the vicissitudes of mass critique. In the words of technologist David Weinberger, this messy transition is a move from

credentialed to uncredentialed. From certitude to ambivalence. From consistency to plenitude. From the opacity conferred by authority to a constant demand for transparency. From contained and knowable to linked and unmasterable.

Linked and unmasterable. That's us. Sounds a little like a gang of primary school kids. But also like a phalanx of rebel warriors. And in that twin identity, we struggle toward a new conception of "the valid opinion." Or, rather, "the *validated* opinion."

This uncredentialed, ambivalent plenitude of opinion is something the elite have been trying to tamp down about as long as we've had communication technologies. Historian Jonathan Rose puts it bluntly: "For as long as writing has existed, the literate classes have attempted to preserve a closed shop through exclusionary languages." In ancient Mesopotamia, he notes, scribes would regularly tag a smug epigram onto the ends of their clay tablets: "Let the wise instruct the wise, for the ignorant may not see." Today's academics aren't so crass about it, but specialized jargon remains, so that outsiders will often get the impression it's not their wits that aren't up to the task, but their ability to use *en vogue* terminology. It is easy to smirk when authority is wrenched from such an abstract elite. Less so when it's wrenched from us, as I learned.

· · · · ·

For several years, and without any supporting credentials at first, I wrote theater reviews for Canada's national newspaper *The*

Globe and Mail. I would attend about three plays a week, rarely publishing the nasty things I scrawled in my notebook to keep myself awake during duller productions. There was a modicum of authority about this task, as one's own opinions, being published in the country's paper of record, were elevated to the level of expert utterance ipso facto. I had no formal training in theater, though, and no abiding obsession with it, either. I had a little learning, and a little curiosity, and that appeared to be enough. Specialists, after all, can kill the interest of a general readership by virtue of their myopia. I was serving, by contrast, as a kind of thoughtful everyman—but one who had the sanctioning stage of the *Globe* from which to voice my opinion. It was fun, and certainly an ego boost.

But then, along came everybody. When did it begin? Perhaps 2008? I remember looking over an advertisement for a play I had reviewed, idly wondering if I'd been quoted in its list of accolades, and I narrowed my eyes instead at a hyperenthusiastic comment that was credited to a certain local blog (how gross, it seemed, to print a Web site address beneath a rave instead of the hallowed, italicized title of a magazine or broadsheet). This struck me as disturbing—maybe even a little disgusting—because that blogger had no authority backing his opinion, and therefore, what was the value of it? Who *cared* what this mouth breather thought about the play? My naïveté went hand in hand with my hypocrisy; there was no real reason why my own opinion mattered, except that it appeared in the *Globe*. It was symptomatic of my own frail position that I felt threatened by online usurpers.

In the case of arts reviews and restaurant reviews, social media and blogs have more or less blown up opinion monopolies. Even while Google and Facebook use intense data mining to monopolize certain kinds of knowledge (kinds useful to advertisers), we also get a proliferation of amateur judgment. The new technology "frees up" the voices of more people, even while it standardizes and controls other kinds of information.

This isn't a new dynamic. For example, while the printing press's most famous child may be the sacred and authoritative Gutenberg Bible, it also allowed, as Elizabeth Eisenstein notes, for

the duplication of the hermetic writings, the sibylline prophecies, the hieroglyphics of "Horapollo," and many other seemingly authoritative, actually fraudulent esoteric writings [that worked] in the opposite direction, spreading inaccurate knowledge.

Benighted medieval worldviews were, in a sense, more available to the literary set of the sixteenth century than they had been to those in the medieval world. (Porn, too, of course; someone ought to write a good book on the explosion of pornography that Gutenberg's invention ignited.) Historians are fond of saying that the printing press eventually gave rise to the clean rationalism of the Enlightenment (and it did), but the machine was indiscriminate and had no particular fondness for the writings of Newton and Voltaire; it was just as good at spreading backward or "immoral" information as forward or "noble" stuff.

. . . . .

By the late 1800s, newspapers opened "correspondence columns" that allowed everyday readers to turn into writers. "The distinction between writer and readership is thus in the process of losing its fundamental character," worried critical theorist Walter Benjamin. "The reader is constantly ready to become a writer," he noted, adding that literary authority had become (shudder) "common property."

After that first occasion when I saw a blogger's words running alongside those of "professional" critics, it was of course as though a dam had broken. Today, press agents regularly give one-person Web sites complimentary tickets to shows in the hopes of eliciting positive buzz. House managers, while asking guests to turn off their cell phones during a performance, implore them to turn those phones back on during intermission and tweet about what fun they're having. Five years after I first noticed the shift, my friends and I declare a movie a good bet because of crowd-sourced ratings. We'll choose one pizza place over another while bumming around Seattle because someone shows us a Yelp page on their phone (we meanwhile roll our eyes at the in-person recommendation of some crank at the hotel). And as I've watched my friends become more reliant on amateur or algorithmic critiques, I've seen them also become amateur critics themselves, seen them eagerly feed the data banks of Yelp and Amazon. Once we get a taste of that sense of enlargement, of mastery over (or at least interaction with) the ocean of information, everybody becomes a pundit. Should we be worried?

· · · · ·

When the elitist-ly named (but Pulitzer Prize–winning) William A. Henry III wrote his most famous book, *In Defense of Elitism,* he took to bemoaning how "the dominant mood of contemporary American culture is the self-celebration of the peasantry." Harsh, yes. At times, the text (written in 1994, just before the "peasantry" got its hands on the "self-celebrating" genius of the Internet) is unabashedly snobbish in its desire to separate the supposed wheat from the supposed chaff. But the elitist impulse is worth looking at a second time because it highlights a position—which is the *absence* of opinion, the *scarcity* of opinion—that we chucked when we went online. And that lack of opinion is something we aren't often encouraged to remember. However, if you believe that some opinions *are* in fact better than others, then you, too, are an elitist of sorts. I remember reading *In Defense of Elitism* at nineteen, with the same sense of shameful transgression that gripped earlier generations when they perused *Playboy.* This was the turn of the millennium, and my university friends were a leftist bunch who would've raised more than their eyebrows at me if they caught me reading *anyone* "the third." Once I said to a particularly severe woman in our group, "Teak furniture is so much nicer than pine," and she wouldn't speak to me for a week.

What would poor William Henry III think of the way I select movies and music online? Instead of seeking suggestions from trusted critics, I browse selections that Netflix offers up "because you watched *Legally Blonde*." (The triviality, the casualness, of our interests and predilections bounce back at us to a sometimes painful extent.) These are algorithmically derived options, based on movies that other people who watched *Legally Blonde* have enjoyed. They are, then, a kind of computerized judgment of their own—a digital version of "Oh, this would be your kind of thing." And more often than not, I'm a little insulted by the portrait of my viewing habits that Netflix tries to paint—and tries to reinscribe. (One friend of mine, David, complains that Google AdSense "treats me like a forty-three-year-old woman because of my personal choices.")

We can presume that in the future much more will be selected by public consensus—and that we'll be vaguely unaware of those selections, too. The computer scientist (and virtual reality pioneer) Jaron Lanier writes angrily against this "invisible hand" in *Who Owns the Future?*:

> If market pricing is the only legitimate test of quality, why are we still bothering with proving theorems? Why don't we just have a vote on whether a theorem is true? To make it better we'll have everyone vote on it, especially the hundreds of millions of people who don't understand the math. Would that satisfy you?

This invisible hand is at work each time you search online. When Google delivers your search results, its algorithm (mimicking an academic tradition) assumes that work that receives more citations has a greater authority. Google, then, privileges search results that are linked to more Web pages and shuttles more popular (that is, relevant) results to page one of the 142 million results for "Glee," for example. Nicholas Carr tells a fascinating story in *The Shallows* that illustrates where this approach can go drastically wrong: James Evans, a sociologist at the University of Chicago, compiled a database of thirty-four million scholarly articles published in journals from 1945 to 2005, in order to assess the number and variety of citations that were used. Had the movement of journals from print to online been a boon for scholarship?

> As more journals moved online, scholars actually cited fewer articles than they had before. . . . Scholars cited more recent articles with increasing frequency. A broadening of available information led, as Evans described it, to a "narrowing of science and scholarship."

The Google-ization of knowledge—that ultimate searchability—creates a great bounty of potential avenues for research. It cannot, however, become a substitute for the strange vagaries of human intuition and creative leaps. We need to insist on a certain randomness, and a large degree of pure, haphazard discovery, in the tools we use to explore our world. The brightest moments of human discovery are those unplanned and random instants when you thumb through a strange book in a foreign library or talk auto maintenance with a neuroanatomist. We need our searches to include cross-wiring and dumb accidents, too, not just algorithmic surety.

And besides the need for accidental connections, there's the fact that some things, clearly, are beyond the wisdom of crowds—sometimes speed and volume should bend to make way for theory and meaning. Sometimes we *do* still need to quiet down the rancor of mass opinion and ask a few select voices to speak up.

And doing so in past generations has never been such a problem as it is for us. They never dealt with such a glut of information or such a horde of folk eager to misrepresent it.

. . . . .

I'm as guilty in all this, as complicit, as the next guy. Looking up a book I'm interested in on Amazon, I can't help noticing that it's the 390,452nd best seller available and that "Josie from Phoenix" thought it was "so boring I threw it across the room." Every product on Amazon—from biscuit tins to baby toys to laptops—comes with its own sales ranking and its own appendage of public opinion. Meanwhile, when a business is too small to manage its own Web site, Yelp often feels like the only way to find its address and phone number; it's a Yellow Pages for people who don't care about Yellow Pages anymore.

Yelp's user base has become quite a mass indeed. When the Web site launched in 2004, it welcomed a modest 300,000 users per month. A few years later, in 2008, that number climbed to 15.7 million users per month. By 2011, the number hit 65.8 million. The curve is not linear; it's verging on exponential: In 2013, Yelp enticed 117 million unique users per month. As of this writing, "Yelpers" have written 47 million reviews of local businesses around the world (mostly restaurants and shops), all entirely without pay. Every second of every day, a Yelp user either receives directions to a business or makes a call to a business through the Web site's mobile app.

The reviews themselves are often insipid or thoughtless, yet their value for those businesses is undeniable. A study published in *Economic Journal* found that when a restaurant's Yelp rating was bumped by just half a star, it correlated with an increased number of patrons, even while all other factors (price, quality of food, service) remained constant. This naturally leads many businesses to create false enthusiastic reviews in an effort to sway public opinion, or at least sway public wallets. Perhaps the surest sign of a Yelp review's significance is the vehemence it can inspire: A restaurateur in Ottawa's famous ByWard Market, for example, was found guilty of libel and sent to jail after she launched an aggressive Internet smear campaign targeted at the author of a critical review.

It's this devotion to, and obsession with, a flattened critical world—one where amateurism and self-promotion take the place of the "elite" critical voices we once relied upon—that leads writers like Andrew Keen (author of *The Cult of the Amateur*) to baldly state: "Today's internet is killing our culture." We get mob opinion instead of singular voices; crowdsourced culture. Consider the Unbound Publishing project, which democratizes the selection of which books get written. Authors pitch ideas to users, who then choose whether or not to fund the writing of said books. "Books are now in your hands," enthuses the Web site. This sounds like a splendid way to produce top-rate *Twilight* porn (and I tip my hat to the creators of such best sellers), but what is the spectrum of books that such an approach will produce, and what sort does it cancel out?

We've proceeded this far with the belief that the broadcasting of our voices is a positive—and certainly it can be—but now our job is to temper that belief with a second question: Might we suffer from opinion glut?

. . . . .

In my years as a critic for various papers, I've reviewed visual art, opera, chamber music, dance, books, and theater. And what I've heard from my fellow critics—during intermission at concert halls or filing out of some independent theater—is a resounding condemnation of the new critical order. "These fucking bloggers," one music writer said to me at a cocktail event, "they swoop in and gobble up all the advertisers, pumping out totally uninformed, *shittily* written drivel. It just makes me wonder why I even bother doing research or interviews." Another veteran critic—from the theater beat—was resigned to the fact that "every time the Internet expands, my job gets smaller. There's less and less space for theater reviews in the paper. Or *paid* theater reviews, anyway." Another simply noted: "*God*, I mean, you read these reviews online and they don't, you know, even know how to use *apostrophes*. Don't people *care* that they're reading stuff written by people lacking a basic grasp of the language?" When everyone becomes an expert, the old experts fade away.

Professional critics have their uses, though—we can aggregate them. Web sites like Rotten Tomatoes (with ten million unique users visiting each month) use masses of data, a crowd of critical reviews, to create an average star rating for films. For reasons best left unexplored, I wrote a review in *The Globe and Mail* of Uwe Boll's 2008 debacle, *Postal*, and Rotten Tomatoes has been using my grouchy opinion of the film ever since. (Naturally, I've not received a penny.) While it might be informative to know that 124 reviews of the Vince Vaughn comedy *The Internship* could be mashed down into a single sulking number—it got 34 percent on Rotten Tomatoes—what does such an aggregation mean for the livelihoods of the critics whose work has been the fodder for the Web site? Who would pay to read a single critic's work when it's already been processed by such a godly and free-of-charge algorithm? Our generation seems to be facing a crisis of critique. We want to know what's best, we want to know where to eat and what movie to see, but we've begun to forget that real opinion, real critique, must always come out of an absence of voices—from a singular subjective viewpoint. You cannot aggregate taste. But in the flood of rating systems and collectivized percentage values, which guide us toward TV shows on Netflix or songs on iTunes, we don't register the loss of that less aggressive suggestion system we always relied on before: face-to-face encounters and singular critics.

I was surprised to find a sympathetic listener in Matt Atchity, editor in chief over at Rotten Tomatoes. I told him I don't love the idea of aggregating critical opinion, saying, "In some ways it's anathema to the whole point of criticism, since it strips the critic of a subjective voice." And Atchity told me, "My worry about that is the one thing that keeps me up at night." I asked him how he thought of his own role in critical debates, and he told me his job is to amass the best opinions in the country for his millions of readers. "Sometimes I feel like I'm the town crier," he told me. "I feel like I'm a herald." Atchity may have good intentions, but the aggregation and flattening of critics still continues at Rotten Tomatoes.

Shall we engineer instead a kind of critical vacuum, an artificial absence of voices, in which comprehensible and highly subjective opinions can prosper?

Perhaps we'll get more of a critic vacuum from companies like Songza, the music-streaming Web site that delivers playlists curated by experts (and occasionally celebrities, from Justin Bieber to New York City's former mayor Mike Bloomberg). Songza is founded on a simple enough premise: If there are twenty-four million songs on the shelf, people become baffled by the panoply of content and fall back on the few songs they already know; access to everything encourages exploration of nothing. Songza's job is to ask you what you're in the mood for (taking a sunny stroll? preparing for bedtime?) and then introduce you to music you didn't know you wanted for the occasion. It's an approach that's working. On any given day, seventy million minutes of activity are logged on Songza. I spoke with the company's cofounder Elias Roman, a twenty-nine-year-old wunderkind from Queens who's found his way onto the *Forbes* "30 Under 30" list. I admit I was relieved to hear his ideas about the future of music. "Some things are easy to crowdsource," he told me, "but when you're interested in constructing a playlist, a coherent whole, it's more than just aggregating a bunch of binaries. I'm saying that there *is* a value to tastemaking."

Tastemaking? The very term sounded antique, wonderfully elitist, coming from the founder of a digital start-up. "We have a desire here to be tastemakers," he continued. "While our algorithms will sometimes offer music that a user has chosen in the past, we have a mandate that the site always brings forward songs you don't know you want yet. There's always going to be both comfort food and something surprising."

Roman's insistence on tastemaking flies in the face of most content providers, who seek only to gratify the known desires of users. And it's an impulse that could go a long way toward countering something that Internet activist Eli Pariser has coined "the filter bubble."

Here's how a filter bubble works: Since 2009, Google has been anticipating the search results that you'd personally find most interesting and has been promoting those results each time you search, exposing you to a narrower and narrower vision of the universe. In 2013, Google announced that Google Maps would do the same, making it easier to find things Google thinks you'd like and harder to find things you haven't encountered before. Facebook follows suit, presenting a curated view of your "friends'" activities in your feed. Eventually, the information you're dealing with absolutely feels more personalized; it confirms your beliefs, your biases, your experiences. And it does this to the detriment of your personal evolution. Personalization—the glorification of your own taste, your own opinion—can be deadly to real learning. Only if sites like Songza continue to insist on "surprise" content will we escape the filter bubble. Praising and valuing those rare expert opinions may still be the best way to expose ourselves to the new, the adventurous, the truly revelatory.

$$. . . . .$$

Commensurate with the devaluing of expert opinion is the hypervaluing of amateur, public opinion—for its very amateurism.

Often a comment field will be freckled with the acronym IMHO, which stands for the innocuous phrase "in my honest opinion" (or, alternatively, "in my humble opinion"). It crops up when someone wishes to say anything with impunity and has become the "get out of jail free" card of public debate. "*IMHO* Mexicans should learn to speak proper English if they're going to work in our restaurants." Can't touch me! Just my opinion!

I've come to see "IMHO" as a harbinger of bullshit. IMHO usually portends a comment that is ill conceived and born of either private prejudice or a desire to trumpet. It's part of a public debate culture in which the "honest opinion" is worthy of publication and consumption not because of any particular merit, but because it is "honestly" the writer's "opinion." In his charming little book *On Bullshit*, the moral philosopher Harry G. Frankfurt offers a useful equation for predicting the manufacture of the manure in question:

> Bullshit is unavoidable whenever circumstances require someone to talk without knowing what he is talking about. Thus the production of bullshit is stimulated whenever a person's obligations or opportunities to speak about some topic exceed his knowledge of the facts that are relevant to that topic.

By this reckoning, haven't we created bullshit machines? In the more than one hundred million amateur travel reviews that fuel TripAdvisor, for example, isn't it likely that our ability to speak publicly almost *always* exceeds our knowledge? The invitation to bullshit, anyhow, is constant.

When I find myself drowning in bullshit—my own and that of others—I think about what it'd be like to sit outdoors at some New York City café, circa 1930, and open a copy of *The New Yorker*, maybe read a book review by Dorothy Parker. What must that have felt like? To draw in a few hundred words of commentary, both discernible and, yes, discerning, completely void of miscellaneous commentary? Wipe away the democratic clamor of "honest opinion" and find beneath a single salient voice. Ms. Parker's "honest opinions" were often briefly stated; she knew the soul of wit ("like the soul of lingerie") was its brevity. When Parker reviewed A. A. Milne's now-beloved *The House at Pooh Corner* she made short work of it: After describing Pooh and Piglet humming in the snow, she demurs, "Oh darn—there I've gone and given away the plot." And nobody jabbered a response. . . . Clarion calls like Parker's weren't smothered by dozens of voices clouding the air with half-baked comebacks.

The review read, the magazine folded and tossed aside, one decides to trust or not trust Parker's opinion and leave it at that. Perhaps on rare occasions a letter is written to the editor (which might be published, if thoughtful enough), but mostly the discussion is one-way and finite. What a lovely thing, to shut up and listen and not broadcast anything back. There's a certain serenity in it and even a kind of light grace.

There has always been an abundance of bullshit. But never before have so many been implicated in the bullshit rigmarole that is public conversation. Before, most of us could point at the bullshitters among us (the politicians and hotheaded pundits) and shake our heads. Today, no such finger-pointing can be allowed because we all swim in the mess. When the armchair philosophers are handed megaphones and the crowd of "honest opinion" starts to overwhelm the trained few, will we begin to think that bullshitting is the only and the natural way to make a call? Or will we engineer opinion vacuums, weed out the bullshit, and separate what is best from what is customary?

CHAPTER 5
Authenticity

But isn't everything here green?

—Dorothy, in L. Frank Baum's *The Wonderful Wizard of Oz*

ANDREW Ng holds a position in the Computer Science Department at Stanford University, where he regularly lectures, year after year, to classrooms of roughly four hundred bright and privileged students. Back in 2008, a video project he launched called Stanford Engineering Everywhere (SEE) let him broadcast base approximations of those classes online. Ng simply stuck a camera at the back of the lecture hall and posted the whole thing on his site, like the world's most boring bootlegged movie. Yet the response—excited viewers kept chatting him up at his Silicon Valley Starbucks—got Ng thinking. There was an appetite for world-class education among those without the means or where-withal to attend an institution like Stanford. How far could that hunger be satisfied? Could the Internet, like other communication advances, allow us (even compel us) to redistribute monopolies of knowledge? Doesn't all information in fact *want* to be free?

Over the next few years, Ng worked out of his living room, developing much of the technology and theory that's used today in "massive open online courses" (MOOCs). Ng was driven by a single question: How can we develop a course that scales to arbitrarily large numbers of students? The answer came in the form of autograded quizzes, discussion forums, a more dynamic lecture recording style, and the startling proposal that peer grading could be as effective as grading from a single authority (if every student grades, and is graded by, five others). In the summer of 2011, Ng set up a new course online, and one hundred thousand students signed up. He did the math in his head: *I'll need to teach a class at Stanford for 250 years to reach that many people.*

The MOOC revolution had begun. On April 18, 2012, Ng announced (along with Daphne Koller) the online learning platform Coursera.org. And Ng's assumptions about that hidden appetite for higher learning proved correct. Latest numbers show Coursera hosts more than five million students who collectively enroll in 532 courses offered by 107 institutions around the globe, including Princeton and Yale.

The advantages of MOOCs are many and clear. Online videos of lectures are massively abbreviated, so an hourlong lecture might become a five-minute video focusing on single action-minded outcomes. Instead of showing a lecturer pacing back and forth in front of bored students, Ng now overlays talk onto visuals that show graphics and handwritten key points—"just the content," as Ng has it. "We also use video editing to cut out the boring bits," he told me. "Some things, like a professor writing for ages on a board, you just don't need to see."

And then there's the data. The piles and piles of data. Coursera doesn't just educate you, it learns from you, too. Every keystroke, every mouse click, is logged in Coursera's rapidly expanding data banks. When a student pauses a video, Coursera takes note; when a student needs more time than usual to answer a question, Coursera logs that, too; it knows when you skip a video, what questions you asked of peers, and what time of day you read the answer. Over its first year or so, Ng told me, "Coursera collected more educational data than the entire field of education has collected in its five-thousand-year history."

To what end? Consider a single programming assignment that Ng devised for one of his MOOCs. Thousands of students submitted a wrong answer—but what struck Ng was that Coursera could scan its data and reveal that two thousand students had made exactly the same mistake in their work. "I was able to create a custom correction message, which would pop up when people had the usual misconception. In a normal class of one hundred students, you won't notice these patterns. So, ironically, in order to achieve this level of personalization, what we needed was to teach a class to one hundred thousand people." (I take his point, though I'm not sure that my definition of personalization is the same as Ng's.) The hope, here, is that mass data analysis will allow Coursera, and other MOOC providers, to create software that personalizes education in much the same way that Netflix, Google, and Amazon already personalize your experience of movie watching, searching, and shopping. Imagine taking a class on twentieth-century literature and receiving helpful advice that "other learners like you" have found useful. The process of intellectual exploration, once highly idiosyncratic, becomes an opportunity to promote whatever material has the highest view count. "Until now," Ng told me, "education has been a largely anecdotal science, and we can now make it datadriven." This reminded me, of course, of Karthik Dinakar, eager to "harden" the soft sciences of psychology and psychiatry with reams of crowdsourced data.

The crowdsourcing of education is further highlighted by Ng's interest in Wiki lecture notes. "At Stanford," he explained to me, "I taught a class for a decade, and writing the lecture notes would take forever. And then, every year, students would find more bugs, more errors, in my notes. But for online classes, I put up a Wiki and invite students to write their own lecture notes; students watch my lectures and create the notes themselves. When you have one hundred thousand students reading and editing the same Wiki lecture notes, the result is a higher quality of text than I could create on my own. Bugs are rapidly squashed." I ask whether the same principle that works for his engineering classes would work for classes on art history or creative writing. Ng pauses for a beat before replying: "I haven't seen any evidence that would suggest otherwise."

Nevertheless, MOOCs and the attendant dematerialization of the education process are creating a certain crisis of authenticity. A large Pew Research Center survey found that most people believe we'll see a mass adoption of "distance learning" by 2020, and many are wondering whether that will brush aside the sun-dappled campuses, shared coffees, and lawn lolling that pre-Internet students considered so essential to their twenty-something lives.

There are also more concrete points to consider. Graduation rates, for starters: Another MOOC godfather at Stanford, Sebastian Thrun (of Udacity), was tantalized for a while by the possibility of bringing Ivy League education to the world's unfortunates, but he later announced in *Fast Company* magazine that less than 10 percent of his MOOC students were actually completing courses. He had become deeply dissatisfied with the MOOC world he had helped to bring about: "We don't educate people as others wished, or as I wished," he said. "We have a lousy product." After signing up nearly two million students for online courses, Thrun despaired at the dismal completion rates; and only about half of those who did complete courses appeared to be learning the material in a meaningful way.

Ng remains hopeful. "I think a lot of content can and will go online," he told me. "The economics certainly work out better that way. But I don't see us replicating the crucial mentor experience, the small-group experience. What I'd like to do is automate routine activities like grading papers and lectures, to free up the professor's time for real conversations. The role of the traditional university is going to be transformed." Meanwhile, the nonprofit enterprise edX announced in 2013 an artificial intelligence program that instantly grades essays and written answers, eliminating the need for a professor's comments.

Ng himself often compares the digital revolution with the original Gutenberg moment, so it follows that he would assume a digital enlightenment is about to follow. "I think we can change the world one day," he says matter-of-factly. "If a poor child in a developing country takes a dozen courses in computer sciences that he didn't have access to before, and then can earn a decent wage, I think in that way we can change the world." Who would deny such an enlightenment? But it may be worth noting here that most Coursera students are not from developing countries. At present, Africa makes up 3.6 percent of the students, while more than a third come from North America and a further third hail from Europe.

Neil Postman, the pioneering technology critic, argues in *Technopoly* that "school was an invention of the printing press and must stand or fall on the issue of how much importance the printed word has." By this measure, Coursera and its ilk are a kind of necessity, a rearrangement of education that's inevitable as our means of communication changes. "For four hundred years schoolteachers have been part of the knowledge monopoly created by printing," continues Postman, "and they are now witnessing the breakup of that monopoly." In the days of Thamus (see chapter 2), the written word was a kind of inauthentic knowledge, and then it became the only true form of knowledge. Is it so unlikely that we're undergoing a similar reevaluation today?

The new knowledge monopoly will feel comparatively abstract, if history is any guide. Advances in cartography, for example, delivered maps that substituted an abstract space for firsthand experiences with natural landscapes; the mechanical clock parsed leisurely "natural time" into regimented sections so that the gong of a church bell had more sway over your comings and goings than your body's own inclinations.[12] Arguably, the larger and more *productive* world that our technologies deliver is simultaneously an impoverished version of the older one—a version that rejects direct experience and therefore rejects an earlier conception of reality that had its own value. We see more, yet our vision is blurred; we feel more things, yet we are numbed. Marshall McLuhan argues that whenever we amplify some part of our experience with a given technology, we necessarily distance ourselves from it, too. (A friend of mine saw those airplanes crash into the World Trade Center while sitting in her living room on the other side of the continent—and thought, against her will, of a movie.)

· · · · ·

Some lens has been shuttered over our vision. We all have felt it. Even as we draw more of the world into our lives, gaining access to people and events we never had access to before, we feel that the things we gather lose some veracity in transit. It happens to me constantly. At my brother's wedding, a hundred of us gathered in my parents' backyard, beneath the glow of trailing paper lanterns strung throughout the trees and white tents. I remember breaking away from the festivities to check my phone, only to find that my friend was posting photos of the very wedding I'd stepped away from: pixelated simulacra of the moment I had left.

The most obvious reason a person would ditch the authentic is, of course, to gain access to a heightened version of dull reality. Enter the promise and wonder of Google Glass, released in 2013, which offers just that—*augmented reality*. The "wearable

....

12. As early as 1370, King Charles V ordered the citizens of Paris to conform their daily activities to the ding-dong of France's first public clock, which he had installed on the facade of the royal palace (the present-day La Conciergerie).

computer" is a (slightly futuristic, slightly dorky) headset fixed with a miniature display and camera, which responds to voice commands. We can tell it to take a picture of what we're looking at or simply pull up Google Images' archive of vintage Hulk Hogan photos because we want to compare the hairdo being sported by that guy on the metro. The company's welcoming Web site smiles: "Welcome to a world through glass." Welcome to augmented (read: inauthentic) reality.

Remember that the Emerald City in *The Wonderful Wizard of Oz* isn't actually emerald. In the Hollywood film version, yes, Judy Garland and her gang traipse through a gorgeous, sparkling town. But in L. Frank Baum's original book, Dorothy and the others are exhorted to put on "safety goggles" to protect their eyes. "If you do not," they are warned, "the brightness and glory of the Emerald City would blind you." Only much later do they discover that it was the green-tinted goggles all along that gave the city its apparent luster. The Emerald City (like the "wizard" behind the curtain) is a fake. "But isn't everything here green?" asks Dorothy. "No more than in any other city," replies Oz. "But my people have worn green glasses on their eyes so long that most of them think it really is an Emerald City."

When we wear emerald glasses with the intention of augmenting reality, we're always giving ourselves over to some authority's vision and relinquishing a portion of our own independent sight.

All our screen time, our digital indulgence, may well be wreaking havoc on our conception of the authentic—how could it not? But, paradoxically, it's the impulse to hold more of the world in our arms that leaves us holding more of reality at arm's length. Coursera.org delivers the world's great teachers to your living room but turns education into a screen interface; a child's cell phone keeps her in constant touch with her friends but trains her to think of text messaging as a soulful communication.

When Walter Benjamin meditated on the advent of mechanical reproduction in 1936, he was already wondering at the uncanny changes that take place when "a cathedral quits its site to find a welcome in the studio of an art lover" or "a choral work performed in a hall or in the open air can be heard in a room." When Benjamin went to the movies—which were now, amazingly, delivering *talking* images on the screen—he saw that they turned rare beauties into easily accessible experiences, all the while degrading the "aura" of that which they projected, their "genuineness." He wrote: "The genuineness of a thing is the quintessence of everything about its creation that can be handed down, from its material duration to the historical witness that it bears." What a strange concern, we might think—*historical witness*. It's that antique notion of actually being there, of becoming richer by being one of the few people or things to have lived in a singular moment, a singular place. Benjamin even worried about the actors he saw on movie screens, noting that "for the first time . . . a person is placed in the position, while operating with his whole being, of having to dispense with the aura that goes with it. For that aura is bound to his here and now; it has no replica." It's a worry, a sensibility, that's nearly demolished by YouTube and its ilk; we aren't trained to care about the *genuineness* of things when digital copies give a zombie-scale crowding of content. This outdated concern for genuineness—for *aura*—requires absence, that one thing we have in short supply. The endgame is this: Without absence in our lives, we risk fooling ourselves into believing that things (a message from a lover, the performance of a song, the face of a human body) matter less. De Beers hoards its diamonds to invent a scarcity that equals preciousness. Perhaps we now need to engineer scarcity in our communications, in our interactions, and in the things we consume. Otherwise our lives become like a Morse code transmission that's lacking breaks—a swarm of noise blanketing the valuable data beneath.

. . . . .

I often feel as though I'm living through a moment of authenticity wobble. Depending on the person I'm talking to—a youth or a senior citizen—my sense of what's authentic, what's *real,* flips back and forth. My own perception of the authentic is caught in the sloshing middle. Perhaps that means I'm less authentic than those who came before *and* those who came after. I dispute both origins. For my peers and me, this confusion is all around us, an ambient fog, though we don't often name it. We look up symptoms on Mayoclinic.org but indulge in "natural" medicine; we refuse to obey any church's laws, yet we want to hold on to some idea of spirituality and read our Eckhart Tolle; we hunch plaintively over our cell phones for much of the year and then barrel into the desert for a week of bacchanalian ecstasy at the Burning Man festival. One friend of mine, who is more addicted to his phone than most, visits a secret traveling sauna once a month located inside a specially outfitted van. He gets naked with a bunch of like-minded men and women and chats about life inside the van's superheated cabin; then he tugs his clothes back on and reenters his digital life. I'm at the point where I won't call one experience authentic and the other inauthentic. We are learning to embrace both worlds as real, learning to accept the origin and aura of things that rain down mysteriously from the clouds.

A prime example is the Google Books project, which has already scanned tens of millions of titles with the ultimate goal of democratizing human knowledge at an unprecedented scale— the new technology needs the old one (briefly) for content; the old one needs the new (forever) to be seen by a larger audience. Screen resolution and printout resolution are now high enough that digital versions satisfy researchers, who no longer need to look at original manuscripts (unless they're hungry for first-person anecdotes). A real Latin copy of Copernicus's *De revolutionibus,* for example, waits for us in the stacks of Jagiellonian University in Kraków; but it, like a fourth-century version of Virgil's work or a twelfth-century version of Euclid's, is handily available in your living room (sans airfare). It's thrilling: our sudden and undreamed-of access to magazine spreads as they appeared in the pages of *Popular Science* in the 1920s or copies of

Boccaccio's *Decameron* as they appeared in the nineteenth century. The old, white-gloved sacredness of the manuscript is rendered moot in the face of such accessibility. Literary critic Stephan Füssel has argued that this means the "precious old book and the new medium have thus formed an impressive invaluable symbiosis." I would only add: For now.

One authenticity must eventually replace the other. But first, this wobble, this sense of two authenticities overlaid, a kind of bargaining.

When Gutenberg published his Bible, he took great pains to please his readers' sense of the authentic by matching his printed work to earlier scribal versions. John Man describes in *The Gutenberg Revolution* an intense labor, geared toward creating a kind of überversion of a handmade Bible rather than something entirely new. Authenticity, or an entrenched idea of authenticity, was key: Three punch cutters worked for four months to create all the punches that would do the printing, painstakingly copying them from a handwritten Bible to replicate the texture of a human touch. (His Bible's 1,282 pages also incorporated accents that scribes had used to indicate short forms of words.) Although paper was readily available—and he did print his Bible on paper—he also imported five thousand calfskins in order to print around thirty "authentic" vellum copies. Gutenberg's Bible, a manufactured masterpiece, claimed traditional authenticity even as it began to rub out that which came before. Yet first came that fascinating moment of flux: In the late fifteenth century, scribal culture and print culture were coexisting, with handwritten manuscripts being copied from printed books just as printed books were copied from scribal ones. The old "authentic" artifact and the new "fake" artifact—for a moment in time—informed each other.

· · · · ·

When we step away from earlier, "more authentic" relations, it makes sense that we also fetishize the earlier "real." Sherry

Turkle argues that, in fact, our culture of electronic simulation has so enamored us that the very idea of authenticity is "for us what sex was for the Victorians—threat and obsession, taboo and fascination." (One can imagine future citizens sneaking into underground clubs where they "actually touch each other.") When I walk through the chic neighborhoods of London or Montreal—when I look through the shops that young, moneyed folk are obsessed by—it is this notion of ironic "authenticity," the refolking of life, that seems always to be on offer. A highly marketable Mumford & Sons–ization. Young men buy "old-fashioned" jars of mustache wax, and young women buy 1950s-style summer dresses. At bars, the "old-fashioned" is one of the most popular cocktails, and hipster youths flock to the Ace hotel chain, where iPhone-toting customers are granted access to record players and delightfully archaic photo booths.

The fascination with the authentic tin of biscuits or vintage baseball cap remains, of course, the exception that proves the rule. The drive toward the inauthentic still propels the majority of our lives. When *aren't* we caught up in a simulacrum? Millions of us present fantasy versions of ourselves—skinnier, richer avatars—in the virtual world of *Second Life* (while our First Life bodies waste away in plush easy chairs). Some even watch live feeds of other people playing video games on Twitch.tv (hundreds of thousands will watch a single person play *Grand Theft Auto* and send cash donations to their favorite players).[13] Meanwhile, in Japan, a robotic seal called Paro offers comfort to the abandoned residents of nursing homes; and the photo- and video-sharing site Instagram is less interested in recording reality and more interested in pouring it through sepia filters. The coup de grâce: Advances in the field of teledildonics promise us virtual sex with absentee partners. All in all, it seems the safety of our abstracted,

---

13. This appalled me briefly before I realized the behavior was no different from paying money to watch a pro athlete play hockey.

cyborg lives is far more pleasing than the haptic symphony of raw reality. Digital life is a place where we can maintain confident—if technically less authentic—versions of ourselves.

It's also a perfect place to shirk certain larger goals. The psychologist Geoffrey Miller, when pondering why we haven't come across any alien species as yet, decided that they were probably all addicted to video games and are thus brought to an extreme state of apathy—the exploratory opposite of the heroes in *Star Trek* who spend all their time seeking out "new life and new civilizations." The aliens "forget to send radio signals or colonize space," he wrote in *Seed* magazine,

> because they're too busy with runaway consumerism and virtual-reality narcissim. They don't need Sentinels to enslave them in a Matrix; they do it to themselves, just as we are doing today. . . . They become like a self-stimulating rat, pressing a bar to deliver electricity to its brain's ventral tegmental area, which stimulates its nucleus accumbens to release dopamine, which feels . . . ever so good.

Wouldn't it make sense to shunt authentic tasks like child rearing, or space exploration, or the protection of the environment, to one side while pursuing augmented variations on the same theme?

. . . . .

Our devotion to the new authenticity of digital experience—the realness of the patently incorporeal—becomes painfully apparent in moments of technological failure. Wi-Fi dies at a café and a fleet of bloggers will choke as though the oxygen level just dropped.

Mostly these strangulations are brief enough that they don't cut us off in any significant way from our new reality. The realness of our digital lives is firm. The breach was just a hiccup. But how invincible, really, is our new reality, our gossamer web?

In 1909, E. M. Forster published a smart little story called "The Machine Stops," in which the web does drop away. In Forster's vision of the future, humans live below the surface of the earth, happily isolated in hexagonal rooms like bees in a massive hive. They each know thousands of people but are disgusted by the thought of physical interaction (shades of social media). People communicate through "plates" (they Skype, essentially), and all human connection is conducted through the technological grace of what's simply called the Machine, a massive networked piece of technology that supplies each person with pacifying entertainment and engaging electronic connections with other people. The Machine does not transmit "nuances of expression," but gives "a general ideal of people" that's "good enough for all practical purposes." When "speaking-tubes" deliver too many messages (e-mail), people can turn on an isolation mode, but they're then flooded by anxious messages the moment they return. Year by year, humans become more enamored of the Machine, eventually developing a pseudoreligion around it in what Forster terms a "delirium of acquiescence."

Humans are warned off of authentic experience. "First-hand ideas do not really exist," one advanced thinker proclaims. "They are but the physical impressions produced by love and fear, and on this gross foundation who could erect a philosophy? Let your ideas be second-hand, and if possible tenth-hand, for then they will be far removed from that disturbing element— direct observation." Inevitably, the virtuosic Machine begins to fall apart, though, and with it the very walls of their micromanaged underground society.

Author Jaron Lanier recalls Forster's story as a message of hope, a fantasy where mankind casts off its shackles (or has those shackles forced off, anyway). "At the end of the story . . . ," Lanier recounts, "survivors straggle outside to revel in the authenticity of reality. 'The Sun!' they cry, amazed at luminous depths of beauty that could not have been imagined."

But in fact Lanier is misremembering here. The underground citizens of Forster's story do *not* climb out from the Machine's clutches and discover the sun. The air above is toxic to them, and when the Machine dies, Forster's heroes are buried alive, catching a glimpse of "the untainted sky" only as rubble crashes down and kills them. There's no revelation; it's a cold, dark death for all of them. The final words spoken in the story are not the euphoric ones remembered by Lanier. The last words anyone speaks are, "Humanity has learned its lesson." Forster is describing a reverse Gutenberg moment. An undoing of the future.

Our own Machine has been similarly threatened before, though we were far less reliant on communication technologies then. On September 1, 1859, a storm on the surface of our usually benevolent sun released an enormous megaflare, a particle stream that hurtled our way at four million miles per hour. The Carrington Event (named for Richard Carrington, who saw the flare first) cast green and copper curtains of aurora borealis as far south as Cuba. By one report, the aurorae lit up so brightly in the Rocky Mountains that miners were woken from their sleep and, at one a.m., believed it was morning. The effect would be gorgeous, to be sure. But this single whip from the sun had devastating effects on the planet's fledgling electrical systems. Some telegraph stations burst into flame.

Pete Riley, a scientist at Predictive Science in San Diego, published an article in *Space Weather* in 2012 stating that our chances of experiencing such a storm in the next decade are about 12 percent. That's a one in eight chance of a massive digital dismantling. If it doesn't happen soon, it'll happen eventually. Great Britain's Royal Academy of Engineering has pegged the chance of a Carrington-type event within the next two centuries at about a 95 percent probability. Such an event almost took place in the summer of 2012, actually, and involved a particle stream larger than we imagine the original Carrington Event to have been. But it just missed the earth, shooting harmlessly over our heads (over the top of a STEREO spacecraft, actually). When we are hit, at any rate, we won't be able to save ourselves with some missile defense system meant for meteors; no missile could halt the wraithlike progress of a megaflare.

What will happen, exactly? Electricity grids will fail; some satellites will break down; aircraft passengers will be exposed to cancer-causing radiation; electronic equipment will malfunction; for a few days, global navigation satellite systems will be inoperable; cellular and emergency communication networks may fail; the earth's atmosphere will expand, creating a drag on satellites in low earth orbit; satellite communication and high-frequency communication (used by long-distance aircraft) will probably not work for days.

I daydream about a latter-day Carrington Event weirdly often, actually. (It's pleasant to have something truly morbid to fix on while sitting on a subway, and if Milton isn't doing the trick, then I switch to other celestial damnations.) Joseph Weizenbaum, the creator of ELIZA whom we met in chapter 3, was able to notice even in the mid-1970s how computers had become as essential to human life as our most basic tools: If extracted from us cyborgs, "much of the modern industrialized and militarized world would be thrown into great confusion and possibly utter chaos." I imagine our transportation and communication systems crashing to a halt, our banks and governments freezing or, worse, misfiring commands. I imagine our refrigeration systems failing and, with them, all our stores of perishable food. Entire power grids blinking off. GPS systems becoming fuzzy to the point of fouling precise military actions. A team of scientists from Atmospheric and Environmental Research estimated that such an event would cost the United States alone up to $2.6 trillion in damage and would take as long as a decade to recover from.

A single lashing from the sun—the most authentic body we

know—could shake our fantastic Machine. The promise prompts us to imagine a moment when our Machine stops entirely (as Forster did). The thought experiment is as enlightening as it is gruesome.

Think of that moment when the fridge shuts off, causing you to realize—in the silence that ensues—that you'd been hearing its persistent hum before. You thought you knew silence, but you were really surrounded by the machine's steady buzz. Now multiply that sensation by the world. Think how cold, how naked, how alone, how awake, you might be. Your own private Carrington Event.

Amazing, how through the creeping years absence could leave us so quietly, so stealthily—yet the return of absence might be so violent a shock.

PART 2

Breaking Away

When from our better selves we have too long
Been parted by the hurrying world, and droop,
Sick of its business, of its pleasures tired,
How gracious, how benign, is Solitude.

—William Wordsworth, *The Prelude*

CHAPTER 6
Attention!

In proportion as our inward life fails, we go more
constantly and desperately to the post-office.

—Henry David Thoreau, *Walden*

THOREAU was right. Whenever I am frustrated, miserable,
thwarted, I'll open my in-box twice as often. But this is not my
in-box's fault. It's mine. My need for distraction is tied to my emotional state. The unopened incoming message is always the best
one; its only content is promise. W. H. Auden described this same
love of forthcoming letters in his poem "Night Mail," where he
meditates on the effect of a mail train running from London to
Scotland:

> *And none will hear the postman's knock*
> *Without a quickening of the heart.*
> *For who can bear to feel himself forgotten?*

In fact, I don't expect to find anything so very extraordinary in
my in-box at all. But the act of calling up the mail itself is a solace. And I can call it up whenever I choose, unlike the locals

waiting for Auden's mail train, who knew they couldn't control its arrival time and so would have put the idea of new messages from their head for much of the day. To check my mail I issue just a click, no commitment at all, and there in the indefinite moment when the e-mail is called forth, I feel the jolt of hope, all in a secret instant where I may have received something wonderful, my gray little life may be changed. Sometimes I think that is the only real moment when I relax, when the world's voice has not quite arrived and I can watch those messages load.

I never used to think this behavior meant I was turning into a stimulus junkie. But then, one day, I forced myself to count the number of times I compulsively checked the status of my in-box. Answer: fifty-two. And what was I looking for there? I go for pure distraction from my duties, certainly, but it's also true that some part of me has an oversize expectation of the messages therein. My eight-year-old self saw the mailman as a bringer of daily gifts, and my adult self is similarly enamored of unopened missives. Psychologists have a term for behavior like mine: "operant conditioning." It's a phrase, coined by B. F. Skinner in 1937, that describes any voluntary behavior that is shaped by its consequences. At its most basic level, operant conditioning implies that a creature will repeat an activity that produces positive rewards (sugar cubes for horses, bingo winnings for humans, and so on). But then comes the insidious part: the "variable interval reinforcement schedule." Studies show that constant, reliable rewards do not produce the most dogged behavior; rather, it's sporadic and random rewards that keep us hooked. Animals, including humans, become obsessed with reward systems that only *occasionally* and *randomly* give up the goods. We continue the conditioned behavior for longer when the reward is taken away because surely, *surely*, the sugar cube is coming up next time. In my case, I need to receive only one gratifying e-mail a month (praise from an editor, a note from a long-lost friend) before I'm willing to sift through reams of mundane messages in the hopes of stumbling on another gem.

I'm not sure I'm as far gone an e-mail junkie as the average American office worker, who in one depressing report was found to be managing her e-mail for a quarter of each day. But let's say I'm enough of a distraction addict that a low-level ambient guilt about not getting my real work done hovers around me for most of the day. And this distractible quality in me pervades every part of my life. I once asked a friend to keep tabs on how many times I looked away from the book I was reading. He told me I glanced away from that particularly good Alan Hollinghurst novel an average of six times every page. The distractions—What am I making for dinner?, Who was that woman in *Fargo*?, or, quite commonly, What *else* should I be reading?—are invariably things that can wait. What, I wonder, would I be capable of doing if I weren't constantly worrying about what I *ought* to be doing? And how content might I become if I weren't so constantly sure that the mailman has my true, far more glamorous life in that bag?

I am certain my childhood brain was less distractible than my adult brain. I have a distinct feeling that I've lost some ability to remain attentive to a book or given task. Who was that boy who read all of *Jurassic Park* in a single sitting in the cloister of his parents' living room? Who was that teenager who, sailing through the Gulf Islands one August, simultaneously whizzed through *Great Expectations* and (sigh) memorized every word of the *Sunset Boulevard* libretto? And who is this frumpy thirty-something man who has tried to read *War and Peace* five times, never making it past the garden gate? I took the tome down from the shelf this morning and frowned again at those sad little dog-ears near the fifty-page mark.

· · · · ·

When the film critic Roger Ebert died, I reread an essay of his from a May 2010 issue of the *Chicago Sun-Times*. In it, Ebert describes his faded love for nineteenth-century novelists—Austen and Dickens and Dostoyevsky. For years, "I would read during breakfast, the coffee stirring my pleasure in the prose." He read them all, spent hours at a go in their complicated worlds. But then he dropped the breakfast and dropped the reading, too. Novels became something one used to fill up transatlantic flights. (And then, once an iPad could be loaded with a few seasons of *Entourage*, they weren't needed there, either.) In the previous year, he had tried to tackle Dickens's *Dombey and Son*, and although he loved the writing, he kept finding himself incapable of continuing. As it was for me with my *War and Peace*, there always seemed to be something else to do. Deadlines, he shrugged. "Tweeting. Blogging. Surfing." Ebert found, as do many other damaged Dickensophiles, that "instead of seeking substance, we're distractedly scurrying hither and yon, seeking *frisson*." Frisson, in this case, is French for "adorable videos of cats trapped in cardboard boxes."

Are the luxuries of time on which deep reading is reliant available to us anymore? Even the attention we deign to give to our distractions, those frissons, is narrowing.

It's important to note this slippage. To remember that those cat videos were not always there. As a child, I would read for hours in bed without the possibility of a single digital interruption. Even the phone (which was anchored by wires to the kitchen wall downstairs) was generally mute after dinner. Our two hours of permitted television would come to an end, and I would seek out the solitary refuge of a novel. And books *were* a true refuge. What I liked best about them was the fact that they were a world unto themselves, one that I (an otherwise powerless kid) had some control over. There was a childish pleasure in holding the mysterious object in my hands; in preparing for the story's finale by monitoring what Austen called a "tell-tale compression of the pages"; in proceeding through some perfect sequence of plot points that bested by far the awkward happenstance of real life.

The physical book, held, knowable, became a small mental apartment I could have dominion over, something that was alive because of my attention and then lived in me.[14] I couldn't perform this magic trick in the company of others, though. I couldn't enjoy reading at all if there was anyone else present. If my parents or brothers came into the living room when I was reading and stationed themselves with a book on the couch opposite, I would be driven to distraction, wondering what was going on in *their* book, and would be forced to leave the room in search of some quieter psychic hollow.

In the purgatory of junior high school, I spent every recess and lunch break holed up in a wooden stall at the school's library, reading a series of fantasy novels called DragonLance, which then consisted of several dozen books (I read them all). And I was not so rare in my behavior, either. Many writers, and also the general population of introverts, will take to reading as a form of retreat. Alberto Manguel relates in *A History of Reading* how the novelist Edith Wharton would escape the stultifying rules of nineteenth-century life by reading and writing in her bedroom exclusively. I had my bullies on the playground, but Wharton had the irredeemable constraints of corsets and polite conversation. In R. W. B. Lewis's biography, she is described as throwing "a minor fit of hysterics because the bed in her hotel room was not properly situated." I'm inclined to agree with Lewis that it wasn't in a proper position for reading. Any devoted reader knows how important it is to have a proper cave in which to commit the act.

But now . . . that thankful retreat, where my child-self could become so lost, seems unavailable to me. Wharton could shut out distraction in her locked bedroom. Today there is no room in my house, no block in my city, where I am unreachable.

At the end of that Roger Ebert essay, he says he decided to

....

14. But the silent reader becomes responsible for the text and, thus, forms an intimate, exclusionary relationship with it. This silent relationship with the text is an invention, not a given: Alberto Manguel describes how, around the year AD 380, the future St. Augustine was astonished, on meeting the future St. Ambrose, to find him reading without moving his lips.

force himself to do the reading that he knew, deep down, his brain wanted and needed. When he gave himself the proper literary diet (and found a room in the house where his Wi-Fi connection failed), "I felt a kind of peace. This wasn't hectic. I wasn't skittering around here and there. I wasn't scanning headlines and skimming pages and tweeting links. I was *reading.* . . . Maybe I can rewire my brain, budge it back a little in the old direction."

Well, I thought, maybe I can, too. Maybe I can "fortify the wavering mind," as Seneca suggested, "with fervent and unremitting care."

I made a list of all my current commitments—work projects and personal ones—and started hacking away at that list while refusing any additions. Eventually, if we start giving them a chance, moments of absence reappear, and we can pick them up if we like. One appeared this morning, when Kenny flew to Paris. He'll be gone for two weeks. I'll miss him, but this is also my big break.

I've taken *War and Peace* back down off the shelf. It's sitting beside my computer as I write these lines—accusatory as some attention-starved pet.

You and me, old friend. You, me, and two weeks. I open the book, I shut the book, I open the book again. The ink swirls up at me. This is hard. *Why is this so hard?*

. . . . .

Dr. Douglas Gentile, a friendly professor at Iowa State University, recently commiserated with me about my pathetic attention span. "It's me, too, of course," he said. "When I try to write a paper, I can't keep from checking my e-mail every five minutes. Even though I know it's actually making me less productive." This failing is especially worrying for Gentile because he happens to be one of the world's leading authorities on the effects of media on the brains of the young—attention deficit is meant to be something he's mastered. "I know, I know! I know all the research on multitasking. I can tell you absolutely that everyone who thinks they're good at multitasking is wrong. We know that in fact it's those who think they're *good* at multitasking who are the least productive when they multitask."

The brain itself is not, whatever we may like to believe, a multitasking device. And that is where our problem begins. Your brain does a certain amount of parallel processing in order to synthesize auditory and visual information into a single understanding of the world around you, but the brain's attention is itself only a spotlight, capable of shining on one thing at a time. So the very word *multitask* is a misnomer. There is *rapid-shifting minitasking*, there is *lame-spasms-of-effort-tasking*, but there is, alas, no such thing as *multitasking*. "When we think we're multitasking," says Gentile, "we're actually multi*switching*. That is what the brain is very good at doing—quickly diverting its attention from one place to the next. We think we're being productive because we are, indeed, being busy. But in reality we're simply giving ourselves extra work." A machine may be able to spread its attention simultaneously across numerous tasks, but in this respect, we humans are far more limited. We *focus*. Author Tom Chatfield points out that our rapid-switch attention strategy works perfectly well when we're checking our e-mail or sending texts about that horrible thing Susan wore last night, but

> when it comes to the combination of these "packets" of attention with anything requiring sustained mental effort, however, our all-round performance rapidly decays. According to internal research from Microsoft, for example, it took workers an average of a quarter of an hour to return to "serious mental tasks" after replying to email or text messages.

The multitasking mind, having abbreviated any deep deliberation it was set to undertake, is therefore more likely to rely on rote information and mechanical analysis. Yet look at the multitasker in action. He or she appears to be a whir of productivity, not some slave to mindless responses. Phone (and cappuccino) held aloft while crossing the intersection—barely avoiding a collision with that cyclist (also on the phone)—the multitasker is in the enviable position of *getting shit done.*

We can hardly blame ourselves for being enraptured by the promise of multitasking, though. The tunnel vision involved in reading, say, *War and Peace* is deeply unnatural; meanwhile, the frenetic pace of goofing around on the Internet has a nearly primal attractiveness. This is because computers—like televisions before them—tap into a very basic brain function called an "orienting response." Orienting responses served us well in the wilderness of our species' early years. When the light changes in your peripheral vision, you must look at it because that could be the shadow of something that's about to eat you. If a twig snaps behind you, ditto. Having evolved in an environment rife with danger and uncertainty, we are hardwired to always default to fast-paced shifts in focus. Orienting responses are the brain's ever-armed alarm system and cannot be ignored.

· · · · ·

This is why a TED Talk lecture, for example, can be even more engaging on your computer screen than it was in person. In a lecture hall, you are charged with mustering your own attention and holding it, whereas a video is constantly triggering your orienting response with changes in camera angle and lighting; it does these things to elicit attention *out of you.* "Televisions and computers," says Gentile, "are crutches for your attention. And the more time you spend on those crutches, the less able you are to walk by yourself."

So now, just as the once useful craving for sugar and fat has turned against us in an environment of plenty, our once useful orienting responses may be doing as much damage as they do good. Gentile believes it's time for a renaissance in our understanding of mental health. To begin with, just as we can't accept our body's cravings for chocolate cake at face value, neither can we any longer afford to indulge the automatic desires our brains harbor for distraction.

"In my opinion," he told me, "we've focused for thirty or forty years on the biological and genetic aspects, which has allowed us to come up with all these drugs to handle attention deficit disorder, but we've been focused on only half the equation. We've focused exclusively on the nature side of things. Everyone seems to think attention problems are purely genetic and unchangeable except by medication."

Given that children today spend so much more time in front of flashing screens (more than ten hours per day, when "multitasking" is accounted for), it would be a willful kind of ignorance to assume so much sparking of our orienting responses wouldn't rewire the brain. "We're now finding," Gentile told me, "that babies who watch television in particular end up more likely to have attention deficit problems when they reach school age. It's pretty obvious: If you spend time with a flickering, flashing thing, it may leave the brain expecting that kind of stimulation." And it's not just infants who need to be protected from such flashes. "We've found that whenever kids exceed the one to two hours of recreational screen time a day the AAP [American Academy of Pediatrics] recommends, levels of attention issues do go up an awful lot."

I stopped him there. "One or *two* hours of screen time a day? That's the recommendation?"

"Yes."

"Does *anybody* meet that standard?"

"Well, no. Probably not."

. . . . .

It's not merely difficult at first. It's torture. I slump into the book, reread sentences, entire paragraphs. I get through two pages and then stop to check my e-mail—and down the rabbit hole I go. After all, one does not read *War and Peace* so much as suffer through it. This is not to disparage the book itself, only the frailty of its current readers. It doesn't help that the world at large, being so divorced from such pursuits, is often aggressive toward those who drop away into single-subject attention wells. People don't *like* it when you read *War and Peace*. It's too long, too boring, not worth the effort. And you're elitist for trying.

War and Peace is in fact thirteen hundred (long) pages long and weighs the same as a dead cat. Each of its thirty-four principal characters goes by three or four different (Russian) names. The aristocrats portrayed often prefer to speak in French, which is odd considering they spend much of their time at war with Napoleon. In my edition, the French is translated only in tight footnotes, as though the translators (Pevear and Volokhonsky) mean to say, "Really? You want us to do *that* for you, too?" There are also hundreds of endnotes, which are necessary to decode obscure sayings and jokes, so I flip about once each page to the rear of the tome, pinching down to hold my place at the front. (Endnotes: the original hyperlink.) It is, manifestly, the product of a culture with far fewer YouTube videos than our own.

In order to finish the thing in the two weeks I have allotted myself, I must read one hundred pages each day without fail. If something distracts me from my day's reading—a friend in the hospital, a magazine assignment, sunshine—I must read two hundred pages on the following day. I've read at this pace before, in my university days, but that was years ago and I've been steadily down-training my brain ever since.

Whether or not I'm alone in this is an open question.

Numbers from the Pew Research Center and Gallup survey suggest that reading levels in fact have remained relatively constant since 1990. Curiously, the largest hit that book reading has taken seems to have occurred somewhere in the 1980s. Then again, the National Endowment for the Arts (NEA) released a massive and scathing report in 2007 that claimed Americans are indeed spending less time reading, that their reading comprehension is eroding, and that such declines "have serious civic, social, cultural, and economic implications." Nearly half of all Americans from eighteen to twenty-four, apparently, "read no books for pleasure."

How are we to square those numbers? Perhaps by focusing less on quantity and more on quality. The NEA report may have come to such wildly different conclusions from those of Gallup and Pew because the NEA is interested in "literary" reading. The report states explicitly, "Literary reading declined significantly in a period of rising Internet use." The NEA was also concerned with quality of reading environment, noting that a third of reading by young adults is accomplished while "multitasking" with other media, including TV and music.

. . . . .

I experienced my first intuition of Tolstoy's larger phraseology around page fifty-eight. Princess Anna Mikhailovna is subtly begging for money from a countess so that she may pay for her son's military uniform.

> Anna Mikhailovna was already embracing her and weeping. The countess was also weeping. They wept because they were friends; and because they were kind; and because they, who had been friends since childhood, were concerned with such a mean subject—money; and because their youth was gone.

In the larger context of war preparations and complex aristocratic maneuvering, I find the sudden vain mention of their vanished youth startling and beautiful (a little comic, too). And this passage has the effect of plunging me into the book properly. For a page or two I am rapt, utterly lost. And then my phone goes off; the miniature absence, and the happiness it gave me, is ended. I want to read, but I stop. I know the distractions are unproductive and I fly to them all the same.

· · · · ·

Humans are not the only animals who behave in unproductive and irrational ways—and it may be easier to observe the arbitrary nature of our behavior if we look to another species first. Consider the three-spined stickleback fish. The stickleback is a two-inch-long bottom-feeder that lives throughout the northern hemisphere. From late April into July, sticklebacks make their way to shallow mating grounds, where the males, as in most mating grounds, get aggressive with one another. Male sticklebacks develop a bright red throat and underbelly during mating season; the coloring is a product of carotenoids found in the fish's diet, so a bright red male, having sourced plenty of food for himself, can be seen by females as a desirable mate, and he can also be seen by other males as serious competition—the reddest male sticklebacks elicit more aggression from other males. The Nobel Prize–winning ethnologist Niko Tinbergen found, however, that male sticklebacks actually attack whatever piece of material in their environment is reddest. (Place a red ball in a stickleback mating ground and the boys go crazy.) They respond purely to the stimulus of the color itself and not to the fish behind the red. A neural network in the male stickleback's head is triggered by the sign stimulus, the color red, and produces instinctive aggression on the spot.

What, I'm now left to wonder, is *my* red? What kind of

stimulus derails my attention against my will; what ingrained tendencies do technologies capitalize on each time they lead me away from the self I hope to fashion? And are they fixed actions, after all? Or are these patterns that I can change?

In the wild, some species have evolved to take advantage of the fixed action patterns of other creatures. The North American cowbird, for example, will lay its eggs in another species' nest, and its young are later fed thanks to the parental instinct of the host bird. Is it possible our more successful technologies have reached a point where they are expert exploiters of our own automatic behavior? The Internet's constantly flashing, amorphous display is an orienting response's dreamboat, after all.

· · · · ·

Another week has passed—my *War and Peace* struggle continues. I've realized now that the subject of my distraction is far more likely to be something I need to *look* at than something I need to *do*. There have always been activities—dishes, gardening, sex, shopping—that derail whatever purpose we've assigned to ourselves on a given day. What's different now is the addition of so much content that we passively consume.

Only this morning I watched a boy break down crying on *X Factor*, then regain his courage and belt out a half-decent rendition of Beyoncé's "Listen"; next I looked up the original Beyoncé video and played it twice while reading the first few paragraphs of a story about the humanity of child soldiers; then I switched to a Nina Simone playlist prepared for me by Songza, which played while I flipped through a slide show of American soldiers seeing their dogs for the first time in years; and so on, ad nauseam. Until I shook myself out of this funk and tried to remember what I'd sat down to work on in the first place.

I'm a little like a character from one of Tolstoy's other novels in this respect. In *Anna Karenina*, a few pages are devoted to his heroine's attempt to read an English novel while traveling by train. She asks her maid for a lamp, hooks it onto the arm of her seat, takes out a knife to cut open the pages, and settles in. But the world around her begs her not to leave it.

> At first she could not read. For a while the bustle of people moving about disturbed her, and when the train had finally started it was impossible not to listen to the noises; then there was the snow, beating against the window on her left . . . and the sight of the guard, who passed through the carriage.

Eventually, the clamor around her adopts a sameness—"the same jolting and knocking, the same beating of the snow on the window-pane, the same rapid changes from steaming heat to cold, and back again to heat . . . at last Anna began to read and to follow what she read." Anna begins to read not because her environment has stopped shifting, but because it is the same quality of shift, and her brain can now ignore it.

> Anna read and understood, but it was unpleasant to her to read, that is, to follow the reflection of other people's lives. She was too eager to live herself.

So, with me; the frisson of the Internet eventually blurs into a dull white roar, and I can return to my book again, sated. And so with me, my mind is jacked up by then to the point where staring at black lines feels ridiculous; there is so much living to live. I'm up and bouncing around after a few pages, realigning books on the shelf, dusting the blinds.

If I'm going to break from our culture of distraction, I'm going to need practical advice, not just depressing statistics. To that end, I switch gears and decide to stop talking to scientists for a while; I need to talk to someone who deals with attention and productivity in the so-called real world. Someone with a big smile and tailored suits such as organizational guru Peter Bregman. He runs a global consulting firm that gets CEOs to unleash the potential of their workers, and he's also the author of the acclaimed business book *18 Minutes,* which counsels readers to take a minute out of every work hour (plus five minutes at the start and end of the day) to do nothing but set an intention.

Bregman told me he sets his watch to beep every hour as a reminder that it's time to right his course again. This sort of advice—so simple, so obvious—is the kind I usually delete from my memory banks immediately, telling myself that my problems are more complicated than that. (Besides, weren't those watch beeps actually distractions in themselves?) But when I spoke with him, it became clear that his ideas actually *were* a complete departure from the place I'd drifted into. And that disturbed me even more: I saw that I'd swerved so far from what I knew to be sensible behavior.

Aside from the intention setting, Bregman counsels no more than three e-mail check-ins a day. This notion of batch processing was anathema to someone like me, used to checking my in-box so constantly, particularly when my work feels stuck. "It's incredibly inefficient to switch back and forth," said Bregman, echoing every scientist I'd spoken to on multitasking. "Besides, e-mail is, actually, just about the least efficient mode of conversation you can have. And what we know about multitasking is that, frankly, you can't. You just derail."

"I just always feel I'm missing something important," I said.

"And that's precisely why we lose hours every day—that fear." And sure, fear seems a good emotion to describe my state of distraction—that anxious fear that I *ought* to be doing something else (or that my life ought to have *arrived* somewhere else by now). Bregman argues that it's people who can get ahead of that fear who end up excelling in the business world that he spends his own days in. "I think everyone is more distractible today than we used to be. It's a very hard thing to fix. And as people become more distracted, we know they're actually doing less, getting less done. Your efforts just *leak out*. And those who aren't—aren't *leaking*—are going to be the most successful."

I hate that I leak. But there's a religious certainty required in order to devote yourself to one thing while cutting off the rest of the world—and that I am short on. So much of our work is an act of faith, in the end. We don't *know* that the in-box is emergency-free, we don't *know* that the work we're doing is the work we *ought* to be doing. But we can't move forward in a sane way without having some faith in the moment we've committed to. "You need to decide that things don't matter as much as you might think they matter," Bregman suggested as I told him about my flitting ways. And that made me think there might be a connection between the responsibility-free days of my youth and that earlier self's ability to concentrate. My young self had nowhere else to be, no permanent anxiety nagging at his conscience. Could I return to that sense of ease? Could I simply be where I was and not seek out a shifting plurality to fill up my time?

So I made a promise to myself. Every day there would be:

Just three e-mail check-ins
and, yes, definitely
One hundred pages of *War and Peace*.

· · · · ·

Today a friend called and invited me to a rooftop barbecue at his place in Yaletown.

"I would, but I promised myself I'd get some reading done tonight."

A stretch of ten silent seconds. "Well, you're an asshole. If you don't wanna come, you could just tell me you have to wash your hair."

"I'm trying to *read*. I'm just trying to *read* a *book*. And I have to read eighty more pages before I'm allowed to sleep and I—"

"What are you reading?"

"*War and Peace.*"

"For fuck's sake. This whole better-than-the-Internet thing is getting seriously tired, Michael. Seriously. I guess just call when you're ready to be part of the world again."

There is so, so much *else* in the world. But I stayed in another night with my book and grew angrier at its pages. It's torture to stay still; it feels far beyond the powers of my tiny will. I once interviewed the tennis star Milos Raonic, and as we tooled around town in a chauffeured SUV, he told me he'd been trained to move so persistently that staying still now freaked his body out; airplanes were impossible. I told him I knew what he meant, except for me the problem was yoga classes—a still mind freaked me out the same way stillness upset his body. (Plus, I always think someone will steal my shoes when my eyes are closed.)

I took to walking around the apartment while reading, so my brain might think I was on my way to do something else. A few days into that experiment, I met Dr. Sidney D'Mello, from the University of Notre Dame, who has a plan that might allow me to outsource my willpower onto a computer, making a piece of software the guardian of my attention span. I'm definitely listening.

D'Mello can monitor real-time attention by using a $45,000 Tobii T60 eye tracker to see whether your gaze remains fixed on what you're meant to be reading. His program has about an 80 percent chance of being correct when it assumes your attention has wandered and can then prompt you by asking surprise questions about the material or even issuing smart-ass comments designed to reorient focus. When I spoke with D'Mello, he'd been working—through many trials and errors—for more than a year on this project. His next step has been scalability, getting his electronic blinders to work through a laptop's simple webcam instead of through the expensive Tobii tracker. "The plan is that eventually anyone can download the software and it will work by monitoring your eye gaze through your computer's built-in camera. It'll also be sensing your heart rate by monitoring your skin color, and it would monitor your keystrokes, too, if you wanted to focus on writing. I see these webcams being part of a rich learning environment."

There are lots of other ways D'Mello and his team can track your engagement. They track your facial expression through those same webcams, they follow body movements based on sensor pads built into your seat, they time how long it takes you to answer questions. And these various inputs are synthesized so that an appropriate response—an alert, a cajole, a complaint—can be issued to the mind-wandering human. *Et voilà!* Instant attention.

This would seem a little ridiculous if it weren't for the fact that it does indeed work. Forty-eight people were tutored on four biology topics—two topics were delivered with a gaze-reactive computer tutor and two with a computer tutor that didn't care *where* you were looking. The results, as written up in a recent paper of D'Mello's: "The gaze-sensitive intervention was successful in dynamically reorienting learners' attention patterns to the important areas of the interface." Learners got more out of the text they were meant to be attending to, and, interestingly, the effectiveness of the gaze-reactive tutor was especially high when the aptitude of the learner involved was higher than average. D'Mello has become especially interested in the attention habits of "high aptitude" versus "low aptitude" learners and received a grant from the Bill & Melinda Gates Foundation to develop intervention systems that spot potential college dropouts who lack the ability to remain alert during mundane academic tasks.

This marks a tidy reversal in attitudes. Eye-tracking studies—using the same type of software D'Mello is incorporating—have proven many times over that when we read online, we read in a cursory way, we scan for information, taking in perhaps 20 percent of the words on a single Web page, often far less. Now it seems likely that we will invite our computers to rebuild our attention—though in line with what strict system of conduct, we must still wonder.

But, then, what if I don't *want* to use an algorithm to read *War and Peace*? I don't want to employ eye-tracking software to keep me reading at some regulated speed of *x* words per second.[15] I do not want to bandage a tech-induced problem with more technology.

It came to me that the kind of attention I wanted to devote to *War and Peace* was the opposite of the robotic eye-gripping mechanism employed in *A Clockwork Orange*. My kind of attention may include long patches of staring out the window. Sometimes I'm thinking about the content of the book, and sometimes I'm staring blankly. Both feel valid. This means, though, that I need even more time set aside for reading, if I'm ever going to finish the goddamn Tolstoy.

· · · · ·

It happened softly and without my really noticing.

As I wore a deeper groove into the cushions of my sofa, so the book I was holding wore a groove into my (equally soft) mind. Moments of total absence began to take hold more often; I remembered what it was like to be lost entirely in a well-spun narrative. Increasingly, there were scenes that felt as overwhelming as the scene where Anna Mikhailovna begged so pitifully for a little money. More moments where the world around me dropped away and I was properly absorbed.

15. That said, eye-tracking software may be useful in keeping long-haul drivers from falling asleep at the wheel. See Olivia Solon's "Eye-Tracking System Monitors Driver Fatigue, Prevents Sleeping at Wheel," in *Wired*, May 28, 2013, http://www.wired.co.uk/news/archive/2013-05/28/eye -tracking-mining-system.

A young, naïve Russian soldier, seeing the French rush toward him, cannot believe he is going to be killed.

"To kill me? *Me,* whom everybody loves so?" He remembered his mother's love for him, his family's, his friends', and the enemy's intention to kill him seemed impossible.

And then, later: After poor, fat, hopeless Pierre is imprisoned for a month in a shed and marched for weeks by a gang of French soldiers, this count, so used to life's luxuries and instant gratification, finds that want, that *lack*, actually increases his pleasure of the smallest things—until he receives his glorious epiphany (which seemed to chime a little with the theme of my own book). Pierre sees

not with his intellect, but with his whole being . . . that happiness lies within him, in the satisfaction of natural, human needs, and that all unhappiness arises not from privation but from excess.

And there was another moment like these, and another. A "causeless springtime feeling of joy" overtakes Prince Andrei as he recognizes a century-old oak that can still bring forth green leaves from beneath its scarred bark; a comet, taken as an omen of death by most, becomes to tearful Pierre a shimmering hope that traversed the vast nothingness of space only to deliver encouragement on his darkest night; Emperor Napoleon takes his troops into the heart of Russia, oblivious to the coming winter that will destroy them all; a distraught administrator in Moscow, abandoning his duties as the city is taken over, orders all the asylum's madmen set loose in the destroyed city's streets. And to all these evocative moments, Tolstoy adds passages of pure philosophy that move beyond the novel's narrative; he takes the time to explain that kings are only the slaves of history, that "the so-called great men are labels that give the event a name, which, just as with labels, has the least connection of all with the event itself." Each time I sat down to read, these big moments, ripe with meaning and sentiment, arrived sooner than the time before, and I lost myself in them with surer gratitude.

It takes a week or so for withdrawal symptoms to work through a heroin addict's body. While I wouldn't pretend to compare severity here, doubtless we need patience, too, when we deprive ourselves of the manic digital distractions we've grown addicted to.

That's how it was with my Tolstoy and me. The periods without distraction grew longer, I settled into the sofa and couldn't hear the phone, couldn't hear the ghost-buzz of *something else to do*. I'm teaching myself to slip away from the world again.

· · · · ·

This reminds me that real thinking requires retreat. True contemplation is always a two-part act: We go out into the world for a time, see what they've got, and then we find some isolated chamber where all that experience can be digested. You can never think about the crowd from its center. You have to judge from a place of absence.

Think of Milton, who took a deep decade off when he graduated from Cambridge (cum laude) to read, read, and read. The year was 1632. Galileo was busy upturning the solar system; construction began on the Taj Mahal; Rembrandt painted *The Anatomy Lesson of Dr. Nicolaes Tulp*; and Milton sat down at his parents' home, first in the village of Hammersmith outside of London and then at Horton (near present-day Heathrow Airport). Apparently, some of Milton's friends were distraught that the bright young scholar was "giving up" his preaching vocation, for we see Milton responding in one letter: "You said that too much love of learning is in fault & I have given up my selfe to dreame away my years in the armes of studious retirement." In the first draft of this letter, Milton includes for his antagonist a copy of his seventh sonnet, in which the poet berates himself for slacking off, too.

> *How soon hath Time the suttle theef of youth,*
> *Stoln on his wing my three and twentieth yeer!*
> *My hasting dayes flie on with full career,*
> *But my late spring no bud or blossom shew'th . . .*

Of course, that "dreame" in which Milton lost himself was anything but unproductive. His studious retirement was a kind of arming period, during which the young scholar mined a prodigious reading list for material that served him the rest of his life and found its way into all his great works.

Steve Jobs touched on the value of such a "dreame" process in the commencement speech he gave at Stanford in 2005. Jobs told the crowd how he dropped out of college, slept on the floors of other people's dorm rooms, and—since he no longer had to subscribe to a preordained course load—took a calligraphy class out of pure interest.

> None of this had even a hope of any practical application in my life. But ten years later, when we were designing the first Macintosh computer, it all came back to me. And we designed it all into the Mac. It was the first computer with beautiful typography. If I had never dropped in on that single course in college, the Mac would have never had multiple typefaces or proportionally spaced fonts. . . . Of course it was impossible to connect the dots looking forward when I was in college. But it was very, very clear looking backwards ten years later.

It seems to me that Jobs, like Milton, had his own arming period, a time when the usefulness of what he was engaged by wasn't called into question. When we're without a particular prescription, we're at ease to discover the things we didn't know we needed to know. Without some faith in that unknown progress, distraction preys on our fears, on our ingrained belief that something—a predator, an exciting new e-mail—requires a nervous shift in attention.

. . . . .

Yesterday I fell asleep on the sofa with a few dozen pages of *War and Peace* to go. I could hear my cell phone buzzing from its perch on top of the piano. I could *sense* the e-mails cramming into my laptop, saw the glowing green eye of my Cyclops modem as it broadcast potential distraction all around. But on I went past the turgid military campaigns and past the fretting of Russian princesses, until sleep finally claimed me and my head, exhausted, dreamed of nothing at all. This morning I finished the thing at last. The clean edges of its thirteen hundred pages have been ruffled down into a paper cabbage, the cover is pilled from the time I dropped it in the bath. Holding the thing aloft, trophy style, I notice the book is slightly larger than it was before I read it.

It's only after the book is laid down, and I've quietly showered and shaved, that I realize I haven't checked my e-mail today. The thought of that duty comes down on me like an anvil.

Instead, I lie back on the sofa and think some more about my favorite reader, Milton—about his own anxieties around reading. By the mid-1650s, he had suffered that larger removal from the crowds, he had lost his vision entirely and could not read at all—at least not with his own eyes. From within this new solitude, he worried that he could no longer meet his potential. One sonnet, written shortly after the loss of his vision, begins:

> When I consider how my light is spent,
> Ere half my days, in this dark world and wide,
> And that one Talent which is death to hide
> Lodged with me useless . . .

Yet from that position, in the greatest of caves, his talent did not waste away at all. Instead, he began producing his greatest work. The epic *Paradise Lost*, a totemic feat of concentration, was dictated to aides, including his three daughters.

Milton already knew, after all, the great value in removing himself from the rush of the world, so perhaps those anxieties around his blindness never had a hope of dominating his mind. I, on the other hand, and all my peers, must make a constant study of concentration itself. I slot my ragged *War and Peace* back on the shelf. It left its marks on me the same way I left my marks on it (I feel awake as a man dragged across barnacles on the bottom of some ocean). I think: This is where I was most alive, most happy. How did I go from loving that absence to being tortured by it? How can I learn to love that absence again?

CHAPTER 7
Memory (The Good Error)

Forgetting used to be a failing, a waste, a sign of senility. Now it takes effort. It may be as important as remembering.

—James Gleick, *The Information*

HENRY Molaison was born in the winter of 1926 and grew up to be a well-groomed, dark-featured Connecticut man whose brain had a habit of flooding with masses of electrical activity. Since a bicycle accident at the age of seven, he suffered from debilitating epilepsy and was visited by a steady string of tonic-clonic seizures (grand mal seizures). Each seizure may have begun with an "aura" phase, in which he would have experienced an intense foreboding and his senses would feel out of whack. This would shortly be followed by a "tonic" phase, in which Molaison's skeletal muscles would seize up and he would collapse to the ground and lose consciousness (here he may have begun moaning or screaming, too). This phase would then be followed by the "clonic" phase, in which his body was racked by convulsions as though electrocuted by an unseen tormentor. The eyes roll back and the tongue is lacerated as the jaw grinds away senselessly. In Molaison's extreme case, this would sometimes occur ten times a day or more. Twenty years of standard treatment produced no relief.

By the summer of 1953, Molaison was a twenty-seven-year-old man with no hope of an ordinary, or even almost ordinary, life. Desperate for a cure, he eventually consulted William Beecher Scoville, a neurosurgeon at Connecticut's Hartford Hospital, who suggested that the patient's hippocampus be surgically removed. And so, on August 25 of that year, Scoville's plan was carried out, with two significant results: Molaison's seizures did subside; and the patient also lost his ability to form new memories.

Stories in the newspaper, what he had for lunch, discussions with loved ones, all these pieces of ordinary information that quietly build for most of us an understanding of the world, our very idea of ourselves, fell immediately through the floor of Molaison's memory and into an abyss. While memories formed in childhood remained intact, Molaison could hold nothing new in the banks of his perforated brain.

Shortly after the operation, a young experimental psychologist named Brenda Milner, then working at McGill University in Montreal, was invited to study the strangely altered patient. Milner had begun reporting on similar cases and was keen to oblige. The meeting would change the course of her life—but also that of the budding field of neuroscience. For the next thirty years, she would visit with Henry Molaison, taking him through a constant series of tests and examinations. At first, there seemed to be little to learn from these tests, since Molaison simply failed to remember anything. For that matter, he never remembered Brenda Milner. How strange for the researcher, to walk through the door at each meeting and introduce herself. To steadily build her portfolio on Molaison and come to think of him as a friend (as she did) while he accrued no records at all of their encounters.

Then one test, seemingly simple, changed everything. Milner brought Molaison to a table and placed before him a piece of paper on which was drawn a perfect star. She then blocked

Molaison's direct view of the paper but allowed him to see the star reflected in a mirror that was placed across the table. Handing him a pen, Milner asked Molaison to reach around the shield and draw the star over the original image, watching his progress in the mirror. The task is difficult for anyone since the mirror plays with our perceptions of right and left, forward and backward. Like anyone, Molaison did a poor job of it.

But Milner had Molaison practice. For three days she returned and had him complete the task thirty times over. And then she noticed an extraordinary change. Although Molaison retained no memory of the exercise (it remained as novel a thing as Milner herself), he nevertheless improved in his ability to trace the star. Finally, he completed the task without error and, looking up at Milner, said in his slow voice, "That's surprising. I thought this was going to be difficult. But it looks as though I've done it quite well." With remarkable simplicity, Milner had revealed that there is more than one system in the brain capable of producing new memories. Molaison may have lost the memory system of his hippocampus, which would have allowed him to remember completing the task the day before, but some other system was still creating muscle memory, motor memory.

After Milner's work with Molaison, a disassociation was established, showing that our brains do not merely house all memories in a single stationary filing cabinet; nor is memory (as was often believed in the 1950s) a vague function of the whole brain. Human memory, we began to understand, is no simple storage device. It exists as a dynamic, a series of systems with information constantly moving between. And changing.

· · · · ·

The more I made room in my life for absence, for solitude, for silence, the more I had time for my memories. Like Henry Molaison, though, and like everyone else, I have a faulty memory, full of holes. I do not enjoy any high-definition recall of infanthood or any revelations about my adolescent years. Rather, the memories that visit me are clouded, obscure. My memories all look broken and untrustworthy. Besides, the really useful stuff—names and dates and facts and figures—is scattered.

I'm baffled by my brain's ineptitude (and deeply impatient with it). The birthdays of co-workers, the career maneuverings of friends, may slip away, revealing me as the unthinking asshole I always thought I was. Some days I forget if I've eaten breakfast; I will literally need to check for a bowl in the sink to confirm whether I need to feed myself. (Yet I remember the flavor of ice cream my childhood buddy once threw a tantrum over—Tiger.)

I've come to think of my memory lapses in terms of a barren mental landscape. What I want is a city full of memories that I can walk through, full of details I can note and well-stocked shops I can peruse. What I have instead is a desert by Dalí, composed mainly of whistling empty space and the occasional melting clock.

I survive on digital cues—my phone is an able secretary, prompting me with reminders and calendars and notes about names of husbands and wives covertly inserted on "contact cards"—but the facade crumbles quickly around Kenny, who knows me better. "How can you ask whether I've seen that movie?" he said the other day. "We watched it *together. Last week.*" I will also regularly forget the names and occupations of friends he's introduced me to multiple times. Kenny sees my lack of memory as a sign that I simply don't care. And, indeed, it's hard to discern between forgetting something and not caring about it. If I cared, surely I would remember.

Does off-loaded digital memory count as caring? I only "know" Kenny's phone number in the sense that I know how to recall it on my phone. And much of my supposed knowledge exists in an equally abstracted state. I find myself living, much of the time, as a happy conduit for information rather than a receptacle. I don't *hold* the information myself and am happy enough to let it reside in a digital state, where I can always get at it if I need to. As King Thamus foretold, I feel all-knowing, but I'm really only managing the illusion of knowledge. Meanwhile, the law of neuroplasticity tells me that each use of a technological memory aid leaves me less able to store information myself. The physicist Haim Harari has written on this diminishing role of factual information in human thinking and wonders what consequences it might have:

> The Internet allows us to know fewer facts, since we can be sure they are always literally at our fingertips. . . . But we should not forget that often in the scientific discovery process the greatest challenges are to ask the right question rather than answer a well-posed question and to correlate facts that no one thought of connecting. The existence of many available facts somewhere in the infinite ocean of the Internet is no help in such an endeavor.

Others argue that future generations will learn to make new connections with facts that aren't held in their heads, that dematerialized knowledge can still lead to innovation. As we inevitably off-load media content to the cloud—storing our books, our television programs, our videos of the trip to Taiwan, and photos of Grandma's ninetieth birthday, all on a nameless server—can we happily dematerialize our mind's stores, too? Perhaps we should side with philosopher Lewis Mumford, who insisted in *The Myth of the Machine* that "information retrieving," however expedient, is simply no substitute for the possession of knowledge accrued through personal and direct labor.

Author Clive Thompson wondered about this when he came across recent research suggesting that we remember fewer and fewer facts these days—of three thousand people polled by neuroscientist Ian Robertson, the young were less able to recall basic personal information (a full one-third, for example, didn't know their own phone numbers). "I've almost given up making an effort to remember anything," he admitted in the pages of *Wired,* "because I can instantly retrieve the information online." Thompson even harnesses Wikipedia in real time, while speaking on the phone, and uses the information stored there to support his arguments. Admittedly I do the same; and I've noticed plenty of colleagues doing it, too. A person just feels *smart* when buttressing a phone conversation with Google-sourced knowledge and shooting it across the line as though it were innately understood. "My point," says Thompson, "is that the cyborg future is here. Almost without noticing it, we've outsourced important peripheral brain functions to the silicon around us. And frankly, I kind of *like* it. I feel much smarter when I'm using the Internet as a mental plug-in during my daily chitchat. . . . You could argue that by off-loading data onto silicon, we free our own gray matter for more germanely 'human' tasks like brainstorming and daydreaming."

Thompson is, of course, not the first to wonder whether he wouldn't be a happier and freer person without the bother of storing mundane information in his head. In a certain sense, we have *always* enjoyed off-loaded memories—and I'm not talking just about history books here. Any long-term relationship (between co-workers or family or friends) involves such a memory system, with individuals each storing a portion of the group's information. Members of the group then remain aware of where the memories they don't personally hold are stored, giving them access to a larger pool of knowledge than they could ever hold themselves. This group memory is called "transactive memory." It allows me to access wisdom from older co-workers or simply access backups of memories I ought to hold myself but have temporarily misplaced ("when's Mom's birthday?"). We constantly judge whether information will be available from an external source in the future, and if it will be, we are willing to forget.

A team of psychologists has reported in *Science* on the degree to which search engines have ramped up our dependence of transactive memory. When a group of volunteers was ushered through a number of memory tests, the researchers found that increased availability of online technologies led participants to recall *where* information was kept (the nodes of transactive memory systems) and participants relied less on retaining the original information itself. The signpost becomes dominant, the fact that it points to drops away. "Where" is prioritized and "what" is forgotten.

"We are becoming symbiotic with our computer tools," concludes their report. "Growing into interconnected systems that remember less by knowing information than by knowing where the information can be found." Importantly, this relationship is not a new "problem," but an extension of that original tendency to off-load and network memory.

> It may be no more than nostalgia at this point, however, to wish we were less dependent on our gadgets. We have become dependent on them to the same degree we are dependent on all the knowledge we gain from our friends and co-workers. . . . The experience of losing our Internet connection becomes more and more like losing a friend. We must remain plugged in to know what Google knows.

As long as transactive memory systems are loose and cumbersome— when it's a bit of a hassle to access the memory inside another person, say—we remain beholden to the memories in our own heads. But increased ease of access (the Google-ization of memory searching) leads to a commensurate increase in transactive memory. Absolute searchability allows absolute amnesia.

· · · · ·

What is the value of *possessing* a memory, after all, as long as the information itself is always at hand? Seneca raised that question two millennia ago when he told the story of a rich man named Calvisius Sabinus. Poor Sabinus (like poor me) was unable to recall even the most famous figures in history—Ulysses, Achilles, Priam—and, like Clive Thompson over at *Wired*, he was ready to use "a mental plug-in." Google was a ways off, so he had to improvise an alternative.

Since what Sabinus wanted was to appear learned among the wealthy and cultured men he socialized with, his priority was *access* to knowledge rather than personal possession of facts. So he purchased slaves (at the cost of one hundred thousand sesterii apiece) to hold the information for him. One slave memorized the work of Homer; another knew all of Hesiod; nine more slaves were assigned to the lyric poets. Sabinus had constructed for himself a ramshackle, flesh-and-blood search engine, allowing him to access poetry he could not remember himself and then repeat it to his guests as though it had sprung from his own memory:

> Having thus made up his family, he was continually making entertainments, and impertinently troubling his guests with his second-hand learning; for he had always someone at his feet to prompt him every now and then with verses.

While his company may have rolled their eyes, Sabinus himself thought this was an elegant solution to his problem; he claimed that since the slaves were part of his property, their knowledge was his as well. This, naturally, left him open to ridicule by his less sluggish friends. One fellow, Satellius Quadratus, witnessed Sabinus's Google-slave display and told him he'd be a fine wrestler. Sabinus was, in fact, a sickly man and answered, "How can I? I can scarcely stay alive now."

"Don't say that, I implore you," replied Satellius. "Think how many perfectly healthy slaves you have."

· · · · ·

No matter how rich we are, none of us can purchase for ourselves a fine mind. Clive Thompson may believe that the "perfect recall of silicon memory can be an enormous boon to thinking." But that's true only if we consider the act of thinking to be mainly the assemblage of collected facts. I'm guessing those dinner guests at Sabinus's place weren't fooled by his off-loaded memory. Why, then, are we?

Of course, we've always jerry-rigged ways to bookmark our memories; the longing to Google long predated the technology. Charles Seife, a professor of journalism at New York University, saw in his personal library a crude attempt to bolster his brainwork:

> Every dog-eared page represents a hole in my memory. Instead of trying to memorize a passage in the book or remember an important statistic, I took an easier path, storing the location of the desirable memory instead of the memory itself. Every dog-ear is a meta-memory, a pointer to an idea I wanted to retain but was too lazy to memorize.

Seife makes an important point here. The Internet is only one instance of our dog-eared recall system. Every table of contents, every index, every card catalog, is a concession to the limits of human memory.[16] Writing itself is the most unabashed of our helpers; it excuses us constantly from storing information ourselves. Remember that in the oral culture that King Thamus bade adieu, a person's ability to think was dictated by his or her capacity to hold information at a personal level; knowledge stopped where a person's memory stopped. Wisdom, too, was measured by memory. We abhor that limitation, though, and have been in the business of off-loading more and more human memory for centuries. Clearly we aren't about to drop such help, especially as

....

16. As Elizabeth Eisenstein points out, indexes, tables of contents, and the like were not natural to printed books, but evolved over time. Even alphabetical order (*a* to *z*) is of course an invention and a direct result of the printing revolution. (See Eisenstein's *The Printing Press as an Agent of Change,* 71.)

the store of human knowledge expands. So what we're really dealing with is a question of attitude. Has the Internet turned a helpful tactic into a monostrategy? Seife continues:

> As the Web grew, my browsers began to bloat with bookmarked Web sites. And as search engines matured, I stopped bothering even with bookmarks; I soon relied on AltaVista, HotBot, and then Google to help me find—and recall—ideas. My meta-memories, my pointers to ideas, started being replaced by meta-meta-memories, by pointers to pointers to data. Each day, my brain fills with these quasi-memories, with pointers, and with pointers to pointers to pointers, each one a dusty IOU sitting where a fact or idea should reside.

As for me, I've grown tired of using a brain that's full of signposts only, a head full of bookmarks and tags and arrows that direct me to external sources of information but never to the information itself. I'd like to know for myself when *La Bohème* was composed and what Jung actually said about dreams and where exactly Uzbekistan may be. I want a brain that can think on its own, produce its own connections from a personalized assortment of facts. Because it seems that the largest database in the world—stuffed with catalog upon catalog of information—still lacks the honed narrative impulse of a single human mind.

· · · · ·

In ancient Rome and Athens, individuals began employing the highly personalized "method of loci" to draw more external information inside their heads and keep it ordered there. Essentially an elaborate mnemonic device, the method involves the construction in one's mind of a detailed building—sometimes called a "memory palace"—inside which memories can then be "placed." If you have a thorough memory of the house you grew up in, for example, you can place a series of memories on the doorstep, along the staircase, and inside your bedroom. As you mentally travel through the fixed image of your childhood home, pieces of furniture or other details will then trigger the stored memory. Even in antiquity they knew the value of pointers. Memory champions today still swear by the method.

The attempt to collect a lifetime's worth of information into an organized and manageable interior space appeared again in a Renaissance endeavor—the cabinet of curiosities. Ferdinand II, Archduke of Austria, kept an elaborate collection of painted portraits depicting people with bizarre physical deformities in his *Wunderkammer*; the cabinet of Russian czar Peter the Great housed deformed human and animal fetuses and other biological rarities. Cabinets of curiosities were for the corporeal world what memory palaces were for the mind.

What's interesting to me about cabinets of curiosities and the method of loci is that they are both attempts—devised when the idea of memory existing in "the cloud" would have seemed preposterous—to pull a world's worth of material into a small, navigable space, one that is privately owned. One can imagine the necessary memory palaces growing larger and larger with each generation, wings and turrets getting stapled onto the sides as we attempt to hold ever more preposterous loads of information. Similarly, the cabinets of curiosities buckle beneath the weight of our discoveries. Both endeavors, though, are very different from the dematerialized and unholdable "cloud" memories championed by Wikipedia and Google. To remember, goes the earlier assumption, you must first digest the outside world and carry it around with you.

This assumption pervaded our thinking until very recently. Consider the case of Sherlock Holmes, who described his own prodigious (and pre-Internet) memory in his debut appearance, an 1887 novel called *A Study in Scarlet*.

I consider that a man's brain originally is like a little empty attic, and you have to stock it with such furniture as you choose. A fool takes in all the lumber of every sort that he comes across, so that the knowledge which might be useful to him gets crowded out, or at best is jumbled up with a lot of other things, so that he has a difficulty in laying his hands upon it. Now the skillful workman is very careful indeed as to what he takes into his brain-attic.

Holmes may have taken this approach too far in his own life. (We learn in the first few chapters that the genius sleuth remains willfully ignorant of fine literature and even the Copernican revelation that the earth goes around the sun—he feels that both subjects would "clutter" his mind.) But the point is that Sherlock Holmes *curates* his memory. He's describing something very like the method of loci here. In both cases, memory is seen as a physical, aesthetically defined space. And in both cases, it is assumed that our job is to *choose*, to *select* what is worthy of placement in the palace of our memory. Human minds (Sherlock Holmes excepted) may be messy places and full of error, but it's the honing, the selection of what's worth remembering, that makes a mind great. Our sense of self is derived in part from all the material we carve away. The limits of the human body, and the human mind, too, are the borders that define us.

· · · · ·

Today, the urge to outdo human memory is expressed in our abiding love of computer records.

"Lifeloggers," who account for their comings and goings in online reports, now find that they can enjoy "total recall" thanks to programs like Timehop, an app that mines information from one year prior to today's date and tells users where they went, what they were listening to, and how they were doing on this, the anniversary of "anytime." Data is culled from users' Facebook accounts, Twitter accounts, and Instagram accounts, among others, to create a digital reminiscence that rough and fuzzy human memory simply can't compare with. It is, in the company's own (vaguely morbid) words, "a time capsule of you."

I spoke with the start-up's young founder and CEO, Jonathan Wegener, a Columbia grad (double major in sociology and neuroscience); he lives in Brooklyn, where Timehop's HQ is located. Wegener made short work of my skepticism. But he did so by defining memory in terms of maximal recall potential: "If we could remember everything, we wouldn't have books. Technology is always about helping us out." And, quickly, the miracle of such enormous computer recall becomes a miracle of computer organization. As Wegener put it, "If I've got thirty thousand digital photos that I've taken, there's no way I'm going to sort through them without some help."

There have been negative responses to the way his invention marshals human memory. Search Twitter for "Timehop" and you'll find people asserting that "Timehop makes me hate myself" or "Timehop made me cry" because users' pasts are constantly thrown up at them with a glaring level of fidelity that human memory might have softened. Oh God, moans the unsuspecting user, I really wore that? I *said* that? It's common for Wegener to receive requests for an algorithm that would weed out negative content from Timehop's capsules, but thus far he hasn't gotten around to it.

The cringe effect was most pronounced in Timehop's (since abolished) text message feature. For a brief stint, the app would regurgitate year-old text messages for users, in addition to the photos and tweets. These proved too personal, however. Only 2 to 3 percent of users made use of the text message software, and those who did, says Wegener, often hadn't thought about whom they were texting one year ago: horrible ex-boyfriends and horrible ex-girlfriends. "People just weren't comfortable with it," he told me. "They'd contact us in a hurry and want the feature disconnected."

Wegener himself is deeply committed to lifelogging and feels that "at a deeper level it makes us feel we're getting more out of life. We're fighting mortality. If we write everything down, it'll stay fresh, you know? I mean, we're being pulled through time against our will toward death. But this can make us feel like we lived."

He also sees his creation as a potential bonding agent for friends and families. "There's a subtlety to Timehop that a lot of people don't pick up on," he told me. "All our hundreds of thousands of users are reliving the same day at the same time. It's a movie theater experience—a very collective experience where the record is playing and you can't stop it. So if your family had a barbecue a year ago, you're all going to relive that experience at the same time." But only, of course, if one's entire family is signed into Timehop. As a terminally forgetful person, I accept that part of me desires the assured and algorithmic narrative such software promises. How much of my hole-filled, personally generated narrative would I do away with if I could replace it with such a happily agreed-upon history?

It would be a wonderful thing if our minds could source such information for us and synchronize our histories so effortlessly. But without our gadgets, the vast majority of our lives actually slips away, never to be heard from again. Sometimes this is a deeply frustrating fact of life. Think of how much we live and how much we lose.

An app like Timehop, meanwhile, doesn't just remind us what we've done, it encourages us to step out of the present and devote more time and energy toward the recording process. Wegener's team wanted to see what happened to social media activity after users signed up for Timehop, so they monitored usage of Foursquare, an app that lets people "check in" to physical locations around town (a Starbucks, a department store, a restaurant), creating a record of one's whereabouts over time. The behavior of twenty-two thousand Foursquare users was mapped out—incorporating three months of activity before signing onto Timehop and three months of activity afterward. Fourteen percent of users began checking in twice as often; 39 percent more users began adding comments and photos to their check-ins; check-ins overall bumped up 9 percent. The company's conclusion: "Timehop makes users better." When users understood that they were creating not just abstract records but fodder for future reminiscences that would be automatically retrieved in a year's time, they became more involved and invested in the lifelogging process. Wegener had tapped into a major social media truth: We do it because we're thinking of our own future as a bundle of anticipated memories. When he and I spoke about his own usage of Timehop, Wegener managed to boil things down to a simple core: "It reaffirms me."

Is there a nobler reason to reminisce? When I consider the state of my brain's dusty mechanisms, by contrast, my supposedly miraculous neurons feel like a broken machine, incapable of "reaffirming me" the way Wegener's app can. I'm a wimp on the beach and my own phone is the jock kicking sand in my face. Is there value, still, in a human memory when a computer's can surpass it so effortlessly?

How much abler, how much more proficient, seems the miracle of computerized recall. What a relief to rely on the unchanging memory of our machines.

Albert Einstein said we should never memorize anything that we could look up. That's practical and seemingly good advice. When I off-load my memory to a computer system, I am freed up, I cast off a certain mental drudgery. But what would Einstein have said if he knew how much of our lives, how much of everything, can be looked up now? Should we ever bother to memorize poetry, or names, or historical facts? What utility would there be in the hazy results? Fifty years from now, if you have an expansive, old-fashioned memory—if you can recite *The Epic of Gilgamesh*, say—are you a wizard or a dinosaur?

· · · · ·

The more we learn about human memory, the less it looks like a computer's. As Henry Molaison's experience first showed us, our memories are not straightforward "recall" systems, but strange and morphing webs.[17] Take, for example, your memory of this word:

Inglenook

An "inglenook" is a cozy corner by the fire. It calls up a pleasant scenario, and the word itself is one of the more beautiful words in the English language, which is why I've selected it as something we may want to have stored in our heads. How might the brain accomplish this?

Assuming you are looking at this text (and not listening to it), the first step will be light bouncing off the paper or tablet that you're holding and traveling through your optic nerves, out the back of your eyeballs, and onto the primary visual cortex at the rear of your head. There, individual neurons will fire (like dots of color in a pointillist painting or perhaps a Lite-Brite toy) to correspond with the specific look of the word: "Inglenook." Many neurons, firing together, create a composite image of the word. This sensory information (the composite image) then travels through a series of cortical regions toward the frontal part of the brain and from there to the hippocampus, which integrates

....

17. Tim Berners-Lee indulges in this recall-as-memory fallacy in a coauthored 2012 paper titled "Defend the Web," where he tells the story of Deacon Patrick Jones, who found succor in "memory aids" after a traumatic brain injury. "His very memory is extended into the Internet," the authors enthuse; but this is clearly not so.

that image and various other sensory inputs into a single idea: "Inglenook." The original firing of neurons associated with "Inglenook" may result in a moment of fluttering understanding in your consciousness, an idea that, in itself, lives for only a matter of seconds—this is the *now* of thought, the working memory that does our active thinking. But that brief firing seems to leave behind a chemical change, which has been termed "long-term potentiation." The neurons that have recently fired remain primed to fire again for a matter of minutes. So if a writer decides to fire your "Inglenook" neurons six times in a row (as I now have), the neurons your brain has associated with that word will have become more and more likely to produce real synaptic growth—in other words, you might remember it for longer than it takes you to read this page. (Literal repetition isn't necessary for memories to be formed, of course; if a singular event is important enough, you'll rehearse it to yourself several times and burn it into your mind that way.)

If your hippocampus, along with other parts of your frontal cortex, decides that "Inglenook" is worth holding on to (and I hope it will), then the word and its meaning will become part of your long-term memory. But the various components of "Inglenook" (its sound, its look, and all the associations you have already made with the experience of reading about "Inglenook") will be stored in a complex series of systems around your brain, not in a single folder.

Next week you may find yourself with an accidental time snack, waiting for the kettle to boil, and in that moment, perhaps the word *Inglenook* will float back into your consciousness (because you'll be thinking about a cozy place by the fire in which to enjoy that tea). But when it does so, the sound—"Inglenook"—will come from one part of your brain, while the look of the word—"Inglenook"—will float in from another; the way you feel about this book will be recalled from some other region; and so on. These various scraps of information will be reassembled—by what means, we know not—to create the complete idea of "Inglenook." And (with so many moving parts, it's inevitable) each time you reconstruct "Inglenook," its meaning will have altered slightly; something will be added, something taken away.[18] Our memories, as the psychologist Charles Fernyhough recently wrote in *Time* magazine, "are created in the present, rather than being faithful records of the past." Or as one of the world's leading memory experts, Eric Kandel, has put it: "Every time you recall a memory, it becomes sensitive to disruption. Often that is used to incorporate new information into it."

The same notion came up again when I had a conversation with Nelson Cowan, Curators' Professor of Psychology at the University of Missouri, and a specialist in memory, who quoted Jorge Luis Borges for me:

> Memory changes things. Every time we remember something, after the first time, we're not remembering the event, but the first memory of the event. Then the experience of the second memory and so on.

"He got that basically right," Cowan told me. "There's a process called 'reconsolidation,' whereby every retrieval of memory involves thinking about it in a new way. We edit the past in light of what we know now. But we remain utterly unaware that we've changed it."

Memory is a lived, morphing experience, then, not some static file from which we withdraw the same data time and again. Static memories are the domain of computers and phone books, which, says Cowan, "really bear no similarity to the kind of

---

18. Associations will come into play that shape and strengthen this memory. For example, the "ingle" part of "Inglenook" might be associated in your brain with "ingots," a building material that might be used to build such a cozy corner; "angle," which sounds like "ingle," might be called up, too. And "nook," which the brain already knows, would be activated in order to form the new word; and so on.

memory that humans have." He seemed provoked by the comparison, in fact, and this struck me because so many other academics I'd spoken with had happily called their computers "my off-loaded memory," without considering in the moment how very different the two systems are. Perhaps we're keen to associate ourselves with computer memories because the computer's genius is so evident to us, while the genius of our own brain's construction remains so shrouded. I complained to Cowan that current descriptions of human memory—all those electrical impulses traveling about, "creating" impressions—hardly explain what's actually happening in my head. And he said only, "You'd be surprised how little we know."

What we do know is that human memory appears to be a deeply inventive act. Every time you encounter the word *Inglenook* from now on, you may think that you recall this moment. But you will not.

. . . . .

Charlie Kaufman's film *Eternal Sunshine of the Spotless Mind*—a fantasy in which heartbroken lovers erase each other from their memories—was based on very real research by McGill University's star neuroscientist Karim Nader, whose work on the nature of "reconsolidation" has shown us how dramatically vulnerable our memories become each time we call them up. As far back as 2000 (four years before the *Sunshine* film came out), Nader was able to show that reactivated fear-based memories (i.e., memories we're actively thinking about) can be altered and even blocked from being "re-stored" in our memory banks with the introduction of certain protein synthesis inhibitors, which disrupt the process of memory consolidation. In other words, it's the content that's pulled into our working memory (the material we actively are ruminating on) that's dynamic and changeable. Today, this understanding grounds our treatment of post-traumatic stress victims (rape survivors, war veterans); like the lovers in *Sunshine*, victims of trauma have the chance to rewire their brains.

I wonder if such measures may become more and more appealing as the high fidelity of computers keeps us from forgetting that which our minds might have otherwise dropped into the abyss. Steve Whittaker, a psychology professor at the University of California, Santa Cruz, has written on the problem of forgetting in a digital age. Interviews with *Sunshine*-esque lonely hearts convinced him that the omnipresent digital residue of today's relationships—a forgotten e-mail from three years ago, a tagged Facebook photo on someone else's wall—could make the standard "putting her out of your mind" quite impossible. In a 2013 paper (coauthored with Corina Sas of Lancaster University), he proposes a piece of "Pandora's box" software that would automatically scoop up all digital records of a relationship and wipe them from the tablet of human and computer memories both.[19] Again, we find ourselves so enmeshed that we must lean on more technology to aid us through a technologically derived problem.

· · · · ·

When I was twenty-one—a third-year English major—I was asked for the first time to accomplish the stultifying job of memorizing a stretch of poetry. To my parents, it was shocking that I'd made it that far without learning by heart a few lines of Shakespeare or Browning. (My mother can still, at sixty-six, recite Thomas Hardy's "The Darkling Thrush.") But my peers and I—the first to use calculators in class, the first to think digitally—never needed to bother.

---

19. Without a "Pandora's box" technology, we are required to engage in an active *scrubbing* of digital memory—we must delete contact info from phones, untag ourselves from photos online. Even then, stray digital flotsam seems inevitable. The perfection of silicon recall may now require perfect deletion, too.

That changed when I took Dr. Danielson's seminar on *Paradise Lost*. On day one, and much to our horror, we were tasked with learning by heart the first twenty-six lines of Milton's epic. Each week, Dr. Danielson had us stand and recite the labyrinthine lines en masse. He told us, "This will give you something to run over in your head when you're standing at a bus stop. You'll always have a poem." A dozen years later, my remembrance of those lines is spotty, sure, and cuts off after line sixteen, but it's more clear than any other piece of literature I read at school, or since. Here's what's still coded in the synapses that know to fire:

> *Of man's first disobedience and the fruit*
> *Of that Forbidden Tree, Whose mortal taste*
> *Brought Death into the world, and all our Woe,*
> *. . . [something] . . . Till one greater Man*
> *Restore us, and regain the blissful Seat,*
> *Sing heavenly muse, that on the secret top*
> *Of Oreb, or of Sinai, didst inspire*
> *. . . [something] . . . who first taught the chosen Seed,*
> *In the Beginning how the Heavens and Earth*
> *Rose out of Chaos. Or, if Sion Hill*
> *Delight thee more, and Siloa's Brook that flowed*
> *Fast by the Oracle of God, I thence*
> *Invoke thy aid to my adventurous Song,*
> *That with no middle flight intends to soar*
> *Above the Aonian Mount, while it pursues*
> *Things unattempted yet in Prose or Rhyme.*
> *[something something . . .]*

This patchwork of poetry is embarrassing, is meager, but it is mine. In less time than it took to tap out those lines, I might have called up the entire ten-thousand-line epic on my laptop—and without the errors. So why do I nonetheless love having it there, broken and resting in the attic of my head?

I wanted to know why my old professor had placed it in my brain in the first place. So I tracked down Dr. Danielson and invited him out for coffee. I recognized him immediately when he entered the café, but he walked up to a different man, a younger one, thinking it was I. (Teachers will usually remember only the first couple of classes they teach with any clarity; the rest of us blur into a mass of personalities, no matter how distinctive we may feel and no matter how large an impact that teacher may have had on us.)

Dr. Danielson has been teaching *Paradise Lost* for more than thirty years now, and every class has been made to memorize the epic's opening. I am only one of hundreds, then, walking around with snatches of Milton because of Dr. Danielson. I asked him whether he'd seen a difference in students' reactions to the task over the course of the Internet's advent.

"If only I'd taken notes on that. . . ." He smiled. "I do think my students today are just as capable of memorizing those lines, but the difference is that they feel they're less capable of memorizing now. It doesn't occur to them that they're able to do something like that, in the same way that a person who's never trained for a marathon can't imagine running one. But every year I get the same comments from students at the end of the term—they'll say they didn't want to do the memory work and that they are so glad they were forced to do it. They will tell me that the memorization was the most empowering part of the course. This is never done anymore, I suppose. It's become very typical that, like you, a student will never be asked to memorize poetry."

"What is it that you think it does?"

"It's this idea of 'formation,'" he began. "Memorizing something literally *informs* your mind. It creates neural pathways, yes? You literally internalize it, download something into your brain. You are programming yourself."

It's telling, I think, that when justifying the exercise of the human mind, we so often resort to computer terms such as "download" and "program." I asked him about the moral behind such programming; if we're programming our minds, then the question becomes *with what*, after all. And here Danielson turned away from technological metaphors and toward a religious one that he learned from an old pastor:

> There's a slightly corny saying that has a lot to it: Sow a thought, reap an action; sow an action, reap a habit; sow a habit, reap a character; sow a character, reap a destiny. And I believe that memorizing something is the sowing of a thought.

Here my professor's conversation seemed to be marrying a certain moralism to the work of neuroplasticity researchers (you are what you do). He told me memorization was the act of making something "a property of yourself," and he meant this in both senses: The memorized content is owned by the memorizer and also becomes a component of that person's makeup. "It makes it part of my lived experience in an ongoing way."

It is this notion of internalizing the memorized thing, of *digesting* it, that so differentiates older notions of memory from newer interests in externalized memory. Previous generations may have had memory aids like writing, but those tools worked only to boost (never replace) a deep commitment to brain storage.

The memorized, internalized work can even achieve the status of a kind of swallowed pill. In Manguel's *A History of Reading*, we learn that the second-century Roman doctor Antyllus felt those who didn't digest poetry suffered "pains in eliminating, through abundant perspiration, the noxious fluids that those with a keen memory of texts eliminate merely through breathing."

. . . . .

Marcel Proust, who maybe thought more intelligently about memory than anyone else in history, knew something about the way our strange brains might heal us. He set out to describe the act of reconstructing one's own past in his greatest work, *In Search of Lost Time,* which was given its title (*À la recherche du temps perdu*) not because the past is a misplaced and retrievable thing, but because it is wasted and gone; searching for lost time (*temps perdu*) is an exercise in fiction itself (it is the anti-Timehop). The work is a kind of hopeless, four-thousand-page salvation mission wherein the "rescued" past self is always a work of art. Reading Proust can inspire us to salvage our own pasts from the obliterating winds of negligence, build some creative self from the available material. When we commit ourselves to considering our own past with even a fraction of the care that Proust brings to the table, we ennoble ourselves.

A century later, Proust's work is a powerful lesson in the mutability and creativity of memory that Nader and Cowan speak about. Personal memories like the ones Proust is dealing with are curated. When we tell stories about ourselves, we select the scraps of identity that will live on in an enduring self. And these memories are strung together by sometimes bizarre and precarious means. Consider Proust's most famous description of personal recall, the madeleine scene. His Narrator finds that a single, idiosyncratic sensory experience can be the key that unlocks a lifetime of observations.

> The taste was that of the little piece of madeleine which . . . my aunt Léonie used to give me, dipping it first in her own cup of tea or tisane. The sight of the little madeleine had recalled nothing to my mind before I tasted it; perhaps because I had so often seen such things in the meantime, without tasting them, on the trays of pastry-cooks' windows, that their image had dissociated itself from those Combray days to take its place among others more recent; perhaps because, of those memories so long abandoned and put out of mind, nothing now survived, everything was scattered. . . . But when from a long-distant past

nothing subsists, after the people are dead, after the things are broken and scattered, taste and smell alone, more fragile but more enduring, more immaterial, more persistent, more faithful, remain poised a long time, like souls, remembering, waiting, hoping, amid the ruins of all the rest; and bear unflinchingly, in the tiny and almost impalpable drop of their essence, the vast structure of recollection.

Proust's remembrance is not a cool accounting of one thing after another, but a polynomial, multidirectional experience; we could even call it symphonic in that several voices and understandings emerge to make a single four-dimensional impression. When the madeleine touches his lips, a world of associations, coexistent in several times ("from morning to night and in all weathers"), rises up "like a stage set." It all "sprang into being, town and gardens alike, from my cup of tea." But all this world is itself only a fraction of the objective world Proust's Narrator must have lived in; a screened vision of the actual past, with each element of the memory tied in some mysterious way to the taste-memory housed in the crumbs of that famous little cake.

Human memory was never meant to call up all things, after all, but rather to explore the richness of exclusion, of absence. It creates a meaningful, contextualized, curated assemblage particular to the brain's singular experience and habits. Valuable memories, like great music, are as much about the things that drop away—the rests—as they are about what stays and sounds.

. . . . .

My own earliest memory always returns to me through the senses. For Proust's Narrator, the past sprang forth, pop-up-book style, when he tasted that simple madeleine dipped in tea. For me, there's a certain weight that, if held in my hands, calls forward a landscape inhabited by my four-year-old self.

What is that weight? Or is it a density, instead? Imagine holding a small box of sand, eight cubic inches, and you'll be close. It does no good to have you imagine the weight of a person's cremated remains, though that's what we're talking about. The memory is not concerned with facts. Think of an eight-inch box of sand. That's the weight that brings this memory back. I pick up a melon or a small stack of books and suddenly the memory reveals itself.

I am four years old, standing in a wild yard above the stone shore of Pender Island. That morning, I was happy to take a short ferry ride from the suburb where I grew up, happy to feel big wind tousling my sandy hair as I leaned up against the railing on the deck with my dad. Now the air is mysteriously still and I can hear even dragonflies quite a distance from me in the grass. Enormous cedars lean over me, and the cedar planks of the family cabin make a red brown box on the far side of the yard. It is summer in my memory, and the rubber tire swing is too hot to use (though what season it actually was, I cannot say). The overgrown grass tickles my exposed legs as I move. I am small, but the slugs in the grass are smaller. I've been stalking them with a glass saltshaker I stole from the kitchen. I am killing them all, dousing them in crystals and watching their bodies turn. The adults on the deck, perhaps twenty of them, are busy in their obscure adult world. I am separate from them.

Then an aunt calls me over and I hide the saltshaker in the grass, unsure whether I've been helping or doing evil. I walk silently over to my aunt, who holds a white cardboard box in her hands. She leans over, without stepping down from the raised deck, and places the box in my hands. She says, "It's heavy, isn't it?" And I nod up at her, holding the box above my head, waiting for her to take it back. My aunt lifts the white box from my grip and turns away; I return to my massacre.

I know now what happened next. The adults convened at the opposite end of the deck and scattered my grandfather's ashes at the base of a young arbutus. But that isn't part of the memory. In the memory, I only retrieve my hidden saltshaker and stalk farther into the grasses. I hold the salt in front of me, like a talisman, while I look for more victims.

Perhaps I'll build myself a clever memory palace one day. It seems we all want such palaces—and we'll probably build them far from the quicksand, the vicissitude of lived memory. We'll build them instead with the 1s and 0s of our devices—spires and spires of perfect digital storage. But for now I have that rough-hewn cabin and shaking field of grass.

CHAPTER 8
Hooking Up

All the boys I have ever loved have been digital . . .
I write his name in nothing, he whispers to the author . . .

—Owen Pallett, "He Poos Clouds"

MY friend Dan often spends his evenings searching for sex through the screen on his phone. Like many gay guys I know, he's unencumbered by debilitating prudery or a boyfriend (whereas I suffer from both conditions). He is charming and handsome enough to procure a little action in "the real world" if he wanted to, but the fact is that Dan, like plenty of others, is permanently logged on to one online tool or another designed to help him get laid.

This new frontier may be inhabited by everyone—gay and straight, men and women—but gay guys are the vanguard. Gay men have always looked for sex through a filter. In the past, our hunting ground was limited almost exclusively to designated bars, bathhouses, and vacant parks. Today, that collection of filters includes the windows on our laptops and the chilled display of our phones. Neighborhood pubs—with their cheap beers and costly glowers—are steadily being replaced by chattering arenas in the cloud.

A little while ago, Dan was talking with a guy on a Web site called Manhunt; he'd known this guy (through his online avatar, at least) for two years. Driven to action at last, Dan asked him out for dinner. "Sorry," came the reply, "only interested in hook-ups." Fair enough, thought Dan, and he moved along. A few weeks later, though, he noticed the fellow had changed his profile so it now read, "Looking for a long-term relationship." Dan rallied and asked him out again. This time the guy said he was interested in getting together only if Dan could provide an additional player; he'd always wanted to try a threesome.

Dan related this to me while frowning into a cup of Earl Grey. He might have encountered such erotic flippancy in any number of offline venues. But as we export more of our sex lives online, it seems there's been a correspondent crowding of casual sexual availability (and sexual rejection, too). Since Web sites like dudesnude and Manhunt gained steam in the early 2000s, men like Dan have been able to order in their sex (or be ordered in themselves) as easily as pizza. We are permanently ready.

Nobody who searched for sex in 1994 and then again in 2014 could help noticing the change. But when I sat down to brunch recently with a group of gay men, it seemed especially clear. A wide-eyed description of some rugby player's physique would give way to an image on a Samsung Galaxy, hurriedly passed around the table. Fussing over whether an encounter was a one-night stand or not would devolve into a critical analysis of next-morning text messages. In fact, the entire appraisal of our sexual behavior seemed quite dematerialized—scrubbed clean of pheromone stink, denuded of flushed skin. And in their place: the scentless rationality of a plastic phone.

Another friend, Jack, is so taken by the promise of online hookups that he interacts with apps like Grindr or the "Casual Encounters" section of Craigslist pretty much 24/7. Even at work. We went out to karaoke the other night and, two pitchers in, I got to asking him about the draw. His smile was a strange mixture of unabashed and contrite: "As much as these sites can be racist, ignorant, and sooooooo full of snobs, liars, and jerks, it's fun to give in to the utter superficiality—just have several sexting conversations on the go at once. The pictures are often lies, and the bullshit of it all can be overwhelming. But I got into it because it still felt better than being alone, you know? Sometimes you have to overdose on something, I guess. And it's all been much more *successful* than any of my bar outings. . . ." He laughs. "I mean, it leads to more actual sex."

Yet the abstracting force of the technology at play, its ability to distance us from our desires even as it promises their fulfillment, always seems to assert itself. There was the time Jack agreed to meet up with a "hot, hung, superfit, dominant top" whom he'd met online. The man turned out to be a frail and elderly fellow wearing cowboy boots, jogging pants, and a grad jacket from several decades prior. (Jack declined their engagement at the door.)

Jack tells me a story like that and I laugh at his misadventure. But then, when the night is through and the dark walk home is chilling my thoughts, I wonder what became of that old man in the cowboy boots. Had he pulled on that outfit thinking the accoutrements of youthful vigor would be enough to continue his online pretense? Did he go back to his computer that night and doggedly entice others to his door? And when those young men arrived, did they walk away as Jack had done? Or did they shrug at the difference between slick online promises and damaged warm-blooded reality, kick off their shoes, and make the gray-haired cowboy happy?

. . . . .

Back in 1999, the lustful hero of *Cruel Intentions*, Sebastian Valmont, spoke for the majority when he muttered that Internet romance "is for geeks and pedophiles." But the Valmonts of the gay world are now among the most ardent supporters of online connections. Prudes and libertines both love, for example, that smartphone application Grindr (launched in 2009). The app alerts men to the proximity (and sexual inclination) of other men, not while they're in a seedy bar, but while they're walking their rottweiler or chatting with their mom at a nice café. It's convenience itself: A person's phone is constantly replenished with a dozen miniature photos of smiling faces (or other body parts), and a fellow can click and chat with other guys, note that they're only 110 yards away, and then arrange what was once called "a discreet encounter." This is hardly a fringe activity: More than six million men have the app on their phones, and it's now used in nearly two hundred countries. On a single Sunday in the fall of 2012, for example, Grindr users sent 37,435,829 messages of love, lust, and denial.

Taken together, such Web sites and apps make a permanent bathhouse of our surroundings. Sexual frames of mind once relegated to special environments are no longer thus bound. And so the bathhouse brain, which is primed for immediate satisfaction, becomes our everyday brain. If I'm sitting in a sun-dappled park reading *Sense & Sensibility* and suddenly take up the idea that I'd like some action *right now*, it's only my own starched manners that will stop me.

. . . . .

Gay men are only the first wave. Straight people are quickly remodeling their own sex lives. Along with selling used sofas and renting apartments, Craigslist, the massive, global classified Web site, has lively sections devoted to the proffering of sexual trysts. Neatly divided by orientation, the site's "Casual Encounters" pages overflow with gentlemen declaring themselves "fit, hung, ready to please" and ladies demurring, "Please have good hygiene." Meanwhile, Chatroulette links strangers from Beijing to

Bogotá via webcam feeds—inevitably leading to the ubiquitous Roulette Flashers, men who masturbate before the camera in the hopes of titillating/appalling female viewers (a report from Tech-Crunch found that one in eight users on Chatroulette is broadcasting R-rated content).

These forums may be tawdry and voyeuristic, but even innocuous connections made on Facebook often belie a sexual pursuit (its progenitor, Facemash, was a game in which Harvard students rated their classmates as "hot" or "not").[20] Explicitly or otherwise, mainstream technologies are now integral to the game. Youths send homemade porn to one another via their phones, while apps like Snapchat encourage risqué photo sharing because they promise to automatically delete images (although, naturally, this turned out to be untrue).

This is not a question of simply transferring offline behavior—meeting via newspaper classifieds, for instance, or picking up a stranger in a bar—onto the Internet. Yes, we've turned every new broadcast technology into a beacon for the lonely (the first printed personals were created a mere fifty years after the invention of the modern newspaper), but no, the Internet is not just an extension of what came before. Surveys conducted in 1980, and again in 1992, demonstrated that less than 1 percent of the population was then meeting through newspaper ads. Today, at least one in five relationships begin online. According to a massive 2010 BBC World Service report spanning nineteen countries, nearly a third of us now consider the Internet a decent place to find a mate, and similar Pew Research Center work focusing on Americans in 2013 saw that number rise to 59 percent.

For many of us, the days begin and end with a consoling look

....

20. Even the in-name platonic Web site Friendster.com was founded (in 2002) by a man who later admitted to doing all the work in order to find good-looking girls: Gary Rivlin, "Wallflower at the Web Party," *New York Times*, October 15, 2006.

at a phone or a laptop. We find ourselves on constant alert for connection—and sexual connection is prime among these. Our technologies offer something irresistible: a shortcut between desire and consummation. They grant us twenty-four-hour access to an alternately frustrating and exhilarating pool of sexual potential and a far larger scope of search. Online connections are, in sum, fast food and dire nourishment in one.

After all, absences are difficult, even torturous. And the alternative, the digital world we've erected to fill those absences, is uniquely adapted to excite our bodies and minds. That much is evident in our basic physiological responses. When we receive a text message, our heart rate increases, blood flow to our skin increases; 83 percent of us, according to one study, even hold our breath. (Writer Linda Stone dubbed this "e-mail apnea.") And as Gary Wilson has pointed out, the dopamine rush we get from viewing porn online is often greater than that induced by real sex (or even old-fashioned magazine porn), because all that clicking and scrolling exploits the searching-and-seeking drive that served our hunter-gatherer ancestors so well. Porn sites deliver a never-ending stream of Tabasco sauce and, "as long as a guy can keep clicking, he can keep going, and so can his dopamine."

But amid the smorgasbord of Tabasco-laced sexual broadcasting, emboldened as we are with the possibility of getting what we want whenever we want it, some essential absence has been taken away. How did our erotic lives get powdered into instant coffee? (*Just add desire.*)

. . . . .

In 1965, accountant Lewis Altfest, together with his computer whiz buddy Robert Ross, created Project TACT (Technical Automated Compatibility Testing), a commercial dating service that, like the descendants it would spawn, relied on the inputting of personal information (do you dislike foreigners? would you rather be Einstein or Picasso?). A customer would pay $5 and fill out a questionnaire, which was then run through an IBM 1400 Series computer equipped with an algorithm that let Altfest and Ross find matches for lonely hearts.

They were keenly aware that computer-aided dating could be seen as both nerdy and déclassé, so for months they walked the streets of New York's Upper East Side, scouting for upscale singles. To doormen, they explained they were working on a graduate research project; once shown into the lobby, they made their way to the wall of mailboxes. Whenever one had two different names on it, Altfest and Ross assumed the occupants were single and added those names to their list. "It was a tailored approach," Altfest told me. "And, if I do say so myself, it was a very sophisticated approach."

Once they knew who was rich and single, Altfest and Ross declared their TACT program an "East Side experiment," something that only people living in the right neighborhood could join. "We restricted it to the poshest area in the city, and sent personalized invitations to all the single people there. We said, This is an experiment, and you'd be doing us a favor if you participated. You obviously don't need a date; you're simply helping us out." The normal return on a direct mail advertising program like that is 1 percent; Altfest and Ross got close to 25.

The race to translate human desire into 1s and 0s had begun. At the same time, a group of Harvard kids was pushing Operation Match, which used computers to identify compatible couples from a bank of college students who had self-rated their own attractiveness and intelligence. Every communication technology is harnessed by the horny of the world, but those students with their lists of tech-sanctified lovers were experiencing something quite new. Apparent in the infancy of online dating were the first intimations of a population in love with off-loading romantic decisions to a yenta algorithm. What a strong impulse that would turn out to be: the desire to have one's desires directed.

Emerging as it did during the sexual revolution of the 1960s,

TACT played off fresh, even courageous, social mores. Dating, courtship, and sex were all becoming more liberally defined at precisely the moment when computers were broadening options for interpersonal connection. By the early 1990s, AOL introduced chat rooms where users could cyberflirt; soon after, sites like Match.com created mathematical formulas to pair up singles. The romantic revolution would deliver us from the silencing odds of our old social circles into a (highly managed) crowd of potentials.

· · · · ·

The advent of GPS-enabled phones has made it possible to take the search outside and into real time. To get a picture of the future marketplace for online hookups, I sat down to lunch with Morris Chapdelaine, a muscled and fast-talking man about as far from tech nerd as one can get. Chapdelaine is the executive editor of a new app for gay men called GuySpy (which had just welcomed its millionth user from its HQ in White Salmon, Washington).

Like Grindr, GuySpy allows men to find one another using GPS, but it fashions itself a social network, too, complete with news stories, blogs, and a community of users. It also pushes established privacy boundaries by pulling up mapping systems and pinpointing the exact street corner that your soon-to-be lover is loitering on. It even includes the option of making anonymous phone calls. Midway through our meal, Chapdelaine had his phone out and was flipping through nearby men. "He's cute. . . . *He's* cute. . . ."

The point is unbridled freedom and access, commensurate with the expanding freedoms and access enjoyed by gay men in general. "Gay bars that exist today," said Chapdelaine, "they aren't even trying. They just paint it black, offer some bad drinks. And you know what? They're over. Guys want to go to the nice bars, to the nice restaurants. You want to be able to hang out anywhere with your straight friends. This app lets them do that."

Chapdelaine is on to something: I spoke with Terry Trussler at Vancouver's Community-Based Research Centre, whose latest research compiles surveys from eighty-six hundred gay men. Trussler found that three-quarters of young men are dissatisfied with designated gay spaces, preferring to roam outside village ghettos. Thirty-six percent of those under thirty used their cell phones to find casual sex (compared with 18 percent of older men). According to Trussler's report: "Internet and smartphones, not bars and cafés, have become the main means of connection between men under 30."

Traditionally, when gay men left their ghetto, they were effectively neutered. You couldn't know who was gay at a mainstream venue, so sexual advances became problematic at best and a physical risk at worst. Today, when gay men go out into the larger world, technologies like GuySpy point out the queer potential of any space. In other words, one can make a four-person gay bar out of a forty-person restaurant. But only, of course, if everyone's using the technology. By this light, mobile sex apps could be something more than erotic fast food. Their use could be a revolutionary act, a way for a sexual minority to stake out territory traditionally denied them.

But why stop there? Apps could next inject this revolutionary attitude toward sex—overt, open, casual—beyond gay culture and into the mainstream. The question is, can the bathhouse brain work for straight people (and lesbians)? Would this approach to sex even be tenable? According to Chapdelaine, it's inevitable. He argues that his app is the future, like it or not. "Ten years from now, this is going to be an integral part of everyone's life, gay or straight."

· · · · ·

This brings us to the heterosexual hitch: the female question. Do women *want* the revolution?

In 2011, U.S. neuroscientists Ogi Ogas and Sai Gaddam published their analysis of the Web search behavior of more than one hundred million men and women around the world (eat your heart out, Alfred Kinsey). Ogas says that, indeed, women's preferences are why heterosexual sex culture is so different from gay men's. "Quite frankly," he told me, "a sex site like Grindr shows us what all men would do if women weren't involved." His position seems to be confirmed by examples of Grindr-esque efforts where men aren't involved at all: Qrushr Girls, a lesbian variation of Grindr launched in 2010, attracted a mere fifty thousand users in three months and then failed.

Whatever engineered them, the blockades between women and casual hookups have thus far kept online technologies from becoming overt, mainstream sex sources for straights. Early attempts to replicate Grindr and GuySpy for heterosexuals are platonic by comparison. One app, called Blendr (yes, produced by the folks behind Grindr), is making a go, with more than 180 million members. Except that Blendr seems ashamed of its true intentions; it bills itself as "a place to find friends," which would be a great tag for a location-based social app for kindergarten children, but less so for consenting adults in search of sex.

On Grindr, a photo of a man's naked torso is accompanied by blunt descriptions of his weight, preferred sexual position, and HIV status. When I scour the Blendr site, though, I learn that "Brittany" likes Hugo Boss and the movie *Titanic*; and "Anna" wants to go Rollerblading with a guy who is older than twenty-five. So much for Blendr's casual sex life.

Perhaps future generations of heteros will be more sexually adventurous? There seems to be a growing comfort with *broadcasting* sexual desire, at least. When 606 students were canvassed at a single high school in the southwestern United States, almost 20 percent of them admitted to having sent a sexually explicit image of themselves through their phone (twice as many said they'd received such an image). (On Grindr, too, it is the digital natives who form the largest user group, and it is also they who are most comfortable with enabling the app's geolocation software.) But that's not the whole picture.

Reading media reports of grade-eight children sending one another homemade pornography leads to the gut feeling that digital life must be an invitation to a hypersexed reality. However, gossipy accounts of adolescent sex lives don't necessarily translate to what's going on. Statistics Canada conducted a National Population Health Survey in 1996–1997 (immediately before the Internet's proliferation) and then again in 2005 (after teenagers had gained access to complex online worlds). Comparison of the two shows post-Internet teenagers were actually having less physical sex than their pre-Internet peers. The number of teens who reported having sexual intercourse dropped from 47 to 43 percent. A more recent StatsCan study found that between 2003 and 2012, there was zero change in the number of sexually active young people. In fact, the only significant change is that youths who *are* having sex are now more likely to use condoms. And the average age when we lose our virginity (seventeen) has not changed in twenty years. The next generation, then, may be producing more signals of sex without actually *having* more of it.

What's not clear is whether all this sexual posturing is making us happier and more fulfilled. As we fill in the longing, the absences that characterize so much of history's erotic art, love songs, and poetry, with the constant connection of digital technology, what fine yearnings have we made extinct? Craigslist, sexting, and porn are superb dismantlers of sexual mystery, but I don't know that desire without mystery, without absence, is quite enough for me.

. . . . .

Of course, other kinds of mysteries are ideal grist for the Internet. Consider Toronto-based AshleyMadison.com, which helps its sixteen million users arrange extramarital affairs. If the business of online hookups has a bogeyman, it's Noel Biderman, CEO of the company that owns AshleyMadison and half a dozen other sites that unabashedly satisfy the needs of specific populations—his CougarLife.com, for example, helps young men meet divorcées and single moms; meanwhile, his EstablishedMen.com helps "perfect princesses" find older, wealthy guys.

Their traffic charts the ebb and flow of secret human appetites: Monday morning is the busiest time at AshleyMadison, as disappointing weekends lead to cheating; late Sunday night is the busiest time for CougarLife, as drunken older women (and drunken young bucks) return home, alone, from the bar; and every site promoting casual sex gets a major spike the day after New Year's, as the world's population makes a bleary promise to itself that, surely, it can do better.

While we spoke, Biderman moved about his twelfth-floor office at Toronto's RioCan Complex (a hub of social media, housing outlets of Facebook and LinkedIn, too). He's a smart, charismatic man. His rationale, surprisingly, matches the harm-reduction argument used to justify safe injection sites: Whether you like it or not, this activity is going to happen, so we might as well mitigate the risk. "Before the Internet, most affairs had to be with someone in your circle, someone at work or your sister's husband," he says. "That's way more damaging." We get to the rub pretty quickly: "It's ridiculous that people take these moral stands about it," he told me. "You can't market infidelity. *You*, for example"—he takes a sharp breath—"I can't *convince* you to have an affair; you either will or you won't. I can only convince you to use my platform. These Web sites are just a platform. We're as agnostic as a phone."

I ask him where hookup technology is headed, and he lays out a bold vision. "We're going to have to build something that goes beyond self-representation," he explains, citing the myriad ways our subjective hang-ups keep us from accurately representing ourselves.

Biderman's argument is that we actually get in the way of our own hookups, that we don't know, or won't admit, what we really want. Instead, we should open up access to the minutiae of our lives (your Web search history, that video you e-mailed your dad, the music you listen to) so helpful algorithms can do their job properly.

"If we can use science, use algorithms, to make our relationships more successful, then that's a positive," he tells me. "We need to get over this idea that infringing on privacy is such a problem. Does it matter if a computer knows what you watch on television?"

. . . . .

I don't care whether a computer knows that I've seen all of *Modern Family* twice. But I do care very much whether my love life is crowdsourced. Yet how could it not be, the more I become enveloped by online processes? And if we end up browsing for sexual partners the same way we hunt for a decent sushi joint, will our true sexual potential have been revealed by the magic wand of Grindr and the rest? Or will it have been masked by the static of the medium itself? Will the omnipresence of choice, in other words, block us from the absences that so often fuel our desires?

The Greek word *eros* in fact denotes "want," "lack," "desire for they who are absent." There is some (perhaps antique) quality of our search for intimacy that actually demands the separations that precede our meetings. I'm not arguing for abstinence here, or even for monogamy. But it seems clear that online technologies promote us toward a state of constant intimacy, and that's not necessarily an ingredient in erotic desire.

Here is Simone de Beauvoir on chivalric love: "The knight departing for new adventures offends his lady yet she has nothing but contempt for him if he remains at her feet. This is the torture of impossible love." Tomorrow's lovers will have a hard time understanding that. All their knights will sit, forever, at their feet.

Gay or straight, it's in our sex lives that the distance between online abstractions and our lived experience is most intensely felt. The crowded, sense-depriving focus of an online experience is the opposite of the spare, sense-gorged experience of cruising the sidewalk at dusk. And isn't it often the weird, unaccountable qualities in a person (his Woody Woodpecker laugh, the way she hugs her friends too hard) that draws us to those who aren't our "type"? If, in our online pursuit of love and sex, we lose those intangible signals, will we one day forget their value so completely that future generations—mired in ever more complex variants on this same perma-readiness—will find it difficult to recall that valuable absence for themselves? The world's largest dating site, PlentyofFish, has seen a massive shift from desktop usage to mobile usage—80 percent of their activity is now run off cell phones. And when users make the switch, they discover an intense love of instant feedback and constant gratification: The number of messages they send jumps by a factor of three or four. Mobile users check their PlentyofFish messages an average of ten times every day.

We might grumble to our grandchildren about the days when people picked up lovers from sparsely populated bars with the same antiquarian fustiness that a fifteenth-century scribe must have felt when the printing press spewed forth those millions of bound volumes. And there's a sad, rare quality to this nostalgia: We will lament what was lost for only this tiny moment in time. Few in the future will go looking for loneliness.

· · · · ·

It would be disingenuous to omit my own sexual career from all of this. My experiences are timid, but, like sixty million others, I broke down one lonely evening and created a profile on PlentyofFish. The spotty results bottomed out with an ornery graduate student whose photos were the most generous things about him.

After I'd bought us a couple of coffees, we started walking the seawall bordering Stanley Park and he grew increasingly irate at the confusion of bodies around us. A child in its mother's arms let out a holler of joy when a flock of birds flew by, and my companion pulled a sour face.

"Don't you hate that sound?" He shuddered.

I looked at him. "The sound of children laughing?"

"Exactly." He picked at something in his teeth.

There was a pause. And then, casting my eyes out over the crowd that swarmed the seawall, I gave a little jump and pretended my phone had started vibrating in my pants. "Hello?" I said to nobody. "Really? But I'm in the middle of a date." I looked at him while I held the dead phone to my ear. "Okay," I said. "I'll be right there."

"I think I made a bad impression," he huffed as we hurried back into town.

"No, no," I lied. And a moment later, as he went in for a hug, I looked down at my phone again. "I have to . . ." But all I could manage was to hold up the device as though the thing itself were a vague yet unimpeachable excuse.

Later that week, in a moment of melancholy, I found myself creating the sort of slapdash artwork that nonartists sometimes make. I tore from a book of Pablo Neruda poetry several short love poems, which I then stapled together, making a long scroll of them that I could nail to the wall by my computer. On this scroll I recorded, in thick black marker, the messages I was receiving from suitors on PlentyofFish. Neruda would begin, "Thanks to your love a certain solid fragrance, risen from the earth, lives darkly in my body," and a PlentyofFish suitor would conclude, "Sup, cute pics." The juxtaposition depressed me in a satisfying way, and I kept the thing nailed there to remind me what I was missing.

A week into that staring, I went against my better judgment and made another online date: this time with a guy called Kenny.

Under "Likes" he had listed: *This American Life*; Animation; Climbing. I like those things, too. But by then I had learned to expect that the person I was about to meet had little to do with the avatar I'd made a date with.

We settled on beers at a swank place in Vancouver's Gastown. "Your photos were dark," said Kenny as I sat down. This shocked me because I hadn't considered that others might feel fooled when they met me; somehow, I never thought of my own online persona as a ploy. I could see the man before me adjusting his idea of "Michael" into a breathing, broken creature. Meeting an online acquaintance in person is always an exercise in disillusionment. (Perhaps the photo is old or softly lit; perhaps the baseball cap strategically covers a balding head.) In old-fashioned meetings, you never have the opportunity to indulge in idealized visions of the person until you form them yourself, in a love-addled haze.

Kenny and I, anyhow, chatted over a flight of European brews and a couple of soft artisanal pretzels. About what, I've no recollection. My only distinct memories are: his comment about my pictures; the moment he got up and asked to switch seats so he could make sure some homeless guys didn't steal his bike; the pressure of his hand on my shoulder as we shimmied past each other around the table. And later, out on the darkening sidewalk, a hit of soap and shampoo as we went in for a hug (no kiss) good-bye.

The American media adviser Lyman Bryson told us that technology is always about explicitness. Technologies—and online technologies especially, I think—focus our attention on one cramped view of things. They cut away the "haptic" symphony of senses and perceptions that make up real, lived interaction. The smell of fresh soap, say. Marshall McLuhan, in *The Gutenberg Galaxy*, writes about the garden of senses that we gave up in order to focus on the purely visual business of reading. Maybe we lived a long time in that garden once. Now we trip into it only on occasion, as though it were a strange gift and not the ordinary, real world. There was that brief, heart-thrumming moment with Kenny on the street, though, when I felt something hopeful start up.

Like my entire generation, I seem to be drawn toward the Internet's fluttering promise of connections, and then repulsed by it, in equal measure. And I feel that, in the end, the Internet will win. On my solo walk home—after I left the man I now call my partner—I might have enjoyed the chance to reflect on his charms or run our conversation over again in my head, committing to memory his favorite beer, the color of his eyes. Instead, I clutched the phone in my pocket, hoping for any slight vibration.

· · · · ·

Two Years Later . . .

Since the day Kenny and I met on that simple evening down in Gastown, the world has carried on, churning out newer and faster ways to connect (or feel connected). I am equal parts amazed and disheartened by the yenta services that have come along. One enterprising company sent me a press release announcing a site called Qpid.me, which helps users test relationship waters by sharing verified STD results. Meanwhile, an app has been released in Iceland that allows users to bump phones and check whether or not they're cousins before having sex (Iceland, we are to understand, suffers from a particularly redundant gene pool). I cannot disparage the utility or good intentions behind such efforts. But I can grouse.

As for me and my man, we are now beyond any online help, it seems, enmeshed as we are in the soft machinations of domestic life. The cleverest innovation *we* employ is the concept of "date night," our standing Thursday evening engagement, when the obligations of friends and families are put on hold and we content ourselves with games of Scrabble and walks through the tony neighborhood up the hill where we like to judge the mansions. There's something disheartening about having to schedule "dates" in this way, but the alternative appears to be no romance at all—leave a vacuum unguarded and life fills it with cocktail events you didn't need to be at and episodes of *Veep*.

Date night was instigated after ten months of laughter and fights, when we decided to move in together. We found a place in a 1930s brick walk-up, not too far from the homes of our siblings. Ours is a one-thousand-square-foot apartment with a sizable living room where we both said we could get some real work done: He would draw and I would write. The light was good, the floors were hardwood; we could see a line of smoke blue mountains from the window—past the parking lot and through the crisscross of telephone wires.

For a desk, we lugged home a nine-foot-long kitchen countertop made of solid oak, to which we bolted a set of $10 IKEA desk legs. Monday to Friday we sit alongside each other at this desk (I'm there now). A squat table lamp in the middle quietly marks the boundary between his zone and mine.

So I sit here typing and Kenny sits there sketching. We're not supposed to talk when we're at work (at the desk). We're alone together. We take silent turns filling the teapot and will take breaks to play stupid games we've made up or to walk around the block. But mainly we're sitting here pretending to be alone. I look over occasionally, to be sure of him.

· · · · ·

What was it that brought us together, exactly? An algorithm chugging along on some server, yes. But what beyond that? I want to know what the brain behind PlentyofFish looks like.

And so, one not so important day in August, I ride an elevator twenty-four stories up to the company's spanking-new headquarters. Seventy-four staff members rotate through these rooms, young folk mostly, in T-shirts and jeans, lined up at long rows of computers. In the cafeteria, baskets of snacks are on offer. I'm ushered into a meeting room called "the Elgin Sea," where I wait for CEO and founder Markus Frind.

When Frind arrives, he's roughly what one would expect: a computer geek's physique, bolstered by the quiet confidence of someone who made more money this morning than you will all year.

Frind was crafting virtual tours of real estate developments when, in his off hours, he wrote the PlentyofFish code out of his living room. There was no way of monetizing the site at first, but it seemed a good way to learn some programming skills; he threw the switch on his dating site after two weeks of work.

A few months later, the site was pulling in $1,000 a month in advertising revenue. "I thought, Wow," Frind tells me (though he's not giving me a wow-face). "About eight months after launching it, I was making *three* grand a month and I quit my day job. I didn't hire anyone else, though, until four years later. By that point I was making ten million a year."

The reticence to hire may be explained by the fierce competition of those early days. "There were hundreds of dating companies coming online back then. But now, you know, we can't steal market share from competitors anymore, 'cause there's no one else to kill."

I tell Frind that his Web site brought my partner and me together, thinking he might smile; but he's heard this before. Maybe a few million times. "So how exactly did your software decide to put my picture in front of Kenny's eyes, and vice versa?"

Frind refers to the system as a "black box"—meaning he's not always aware himself of the choices his software is making. But the math comes down to shared interests. If two people share qualities that other successful couples have shared, then Plenty-ofFish's algorithm will assume you should check each other out. I field the old idea that opposites attract, and Frind says, "Yeah, opposites attract and then they attack. We've found that if you share interests, you're twice as likely to stay together."

And most shared interests, he tells me, boil down to a similarity in disposable income. "Income tells us everything," Frind says. "There's a lot of matching that's based on income. And education, too, but that's a proxy for income. I mean, you're not going to match a doctor with a carpenter; we know that if you have a PhD, you won't date someone without a high school diploma."

"Sounds harsh."

"Yeah, but we model on what actually happens. People don't like to hear it, but this is the way the world works."

Other matchmaking decisions are equally strident. "If you're a guy, you're never going to see a girl that's taller than you," says Frind. (He gestures at me and says, "But for gay people we drop that criterion.") Also, men looking to be in touch with women more than fourteen years their junior, or men who use graphic language in their messages, will find their communications blocked. "I looked at a bunch of metrics and was wondering how we could get more people dating online. We saw there was a small group of men just looking to hook up, and the theory was these men were making women leave." (PlentyofFish is especially solicitous of its women, since they make up only 40 percent of their user base.)

By the time we shook hands, I saw Frind as a friendly, businesslike man who captains a ruthless, brilliant, and efficient service. And I saw it was actually up to individuals, then, to draw something meaningful or romantic from the vagaries of Frind's teeming crowd. From a mass of sixty million, draw one person to love. And then, against all odds, make it work. It was more than a little unsettling to see that such a calculated and crowdsourced system had brought us together in the first place.

CHAPTER 9
How to Absent Oneself

Ah, where have they gone, those loafing heroes of folk song, those vagabonds who roam from one mill to another and bed down under the stars?

—Milan Kundera, *Slowness*

FROM the driveway, Douglas Coupland's house doesn't look as if it belongs to a person interested in the future. He lives at the foot of a wooded cul-de-sac, on the side of a big green hill, just a couple of blocks from the house where I grew up. His gravel driveway is shrouded by banks of bamboo, and the house itself—midcentury design—is edged with schools of handmade pottery, the kinds of pieces that friends bring back from trips to the Gulf Islands. I've come here to talk about absence with Coupland because he strikes me as a writer who knows how to live well in the digital world. His books—from *Generation X* to *Microserfs* to *jPod*—deliver portraits of contemporary souls both adrift in their tech-addled world and discovering new meanings, new interpersonal revelations that sometimes reach a comforting, even religious, tenor.

Coffee in the living room. A wall has been bolted over with plastic toy parts so it looks like a motherboard designed to process the zeitgeist. Coupland (fifty-one, with the white and swept-back hair of a medieval herbalist) is searching the room for an answer. I've just asked: "When was the last time you went a day without the Internet?"

"A decade ago," he says at last. "My IT guy screwed up and I was offline for two days in London. But other than that I've been online every day since the nineties."

"You never go offline on purpose?"

Sip of coffee; mini grimace. "I'd go crazy. You remember when Wikipedia had its one-day blackout? It totally crimped my lifestyle." This surprises me, maybe disappoints me a little. Maybe I thought Coupland would tell me that the secret to writing a dozen international best sellers was that he did e-mail only once a week. . . .

He continues: "There have been these little milestones over the years—when I canceled the newspaper, when I started cooking with the Internet, these little things that tell you your brain's been colonized." It's a colonization Coupland likes, though. He Googles about one hundred times a day, and at the moment, he's wearing a black bracelet that tracks his sleep patterns; every REM cycle is nicely charted with multicolored bars.

To Coupland, the colonization presents us with an intellectual paradox—we know everything and we know nothing. Shoveling the Internet into our brains gives us a mental state where "we acknowledge that we've never been smarter as individuals and yet somehow we've never felt stupider." The word he uses to describe this paradox is "smupid" (a portmanteau of "smart" plus "stupid"). Smupid people acknowledge their enhanced intelligence but feel stupid because the info was just *way* too easy to access. There's a *Financial Times* piece he's written that gives an example of smupid thinking: "Last month someone showed me a page of the *Frankfurter Allgemeine Zeitung* and I looked at the words on the paper and I kept waiting for the article to translate itself. I felt *smupid*."

I tell him I'm interested in undoing my own smupidity by trying something drastic—a vacation in the tech environment of my childhood. "I want to take a month off from the Internet," I tell him. "An e-mail sabbatical. I'm also going to leave the phone at home. It's sort of like a reverse Rumspringa."

"Man," he says, squinting across the room. "You couldn't *pay* me to go back in time."

"You don't think there'll be any value in it?"

"Well, maybe. Are you expecting a revelation, though? I mean, you can take a sabbatical from the Internet if you want, but it would be like taking a sabbatical from shoes." I feel foolish, then, and don't know what to say next.

A few days later, Coupland invites me back to talk some more. We sit in a work area off the kitchen this time—amid piles of books and papers, scribbles of ink and cobblings of Lego and hits of primary color buzz the room up with the beginnings of eighty-two thousand ideas. We're into the coffee again and our laptops are facing each other so I get the feeling we're about to play a game of Battleship.

We start talking about Alan Turing and his conflation of human intelligence with computers. Coupland's saying, "You know, it may be that our emotions are just the simplest way to code certain information—" Then there's a rattle outside. A blue jay on the gravel. Coupland gets up to feed the bird through a slat in the window. A moment later, the bird's skirted around to a pond. "Oooh, beauty moment," he says. And we pause the tech talk to watch the jay, whose own opinions shall remain unpublished.

I ask again about absence.

"Well . . . ," he says. "Well, yes, there's beachcombing."

"Beachcombing?"

"I go with Gordon Smith [the ninety-five-year-old painter]. It's our favorite thing on earth, beachcombing. We have elaborate trips. The thing about it is you're walking, it's physical in a nice way, and you're gazing at the ground. Your brain goes into this mode . . . There's one beach with barnacles, another where the Haida people have chucked all their old bones and the ocean has churned them over . . . You do it for an hour or two or three and your brain starts to feel like you've taken the best nap ever. You go nonverbal. To this place without words."

We're quiet ourselves for a beat, and my gaze dodges reflexively back to my laptop's screen. I look up: "You said once that the Internet could make you tired of knowing everything. Were you joking, or being serious?"

"Maybe."

. . . . .

Down the road was that green hill of mine. I still had some shaky memory of feeling at peace there in a way I'd never been since. And so, the next day, I walked the trail alone and took myself partway up the grassy rise. I patted my pockets, thinking I should turn off my phone, until I remembered that I hadn't brought it with me. I lay down with an old-man groan and looked up at the blue above me, tried to imagine billions of phone calls and Web searches flying across the air, leaving colored jet streams, until everything above was a weave of tight connections.

I thought of Kenny, who would be wondering about lunch; and my parents, to whom I should send a "Happy Anniversary" text; editors in Toronto and New York who wanted their updates; and all the messages I needed to send or receive in order to get what I wanted, in order to make sure. . . .

I wanted badly, then, to have some revelation—even kept blinking at the sky, to reboot it. I thought it was *time* for my revelation, that I deserved by now some newfound silence or solitude that would close this book on a happy, even inspirational, lob. I was ready for my personal transformation.

But let me tell you the truth, instead.

If you look closely at the loss of lack, the end of absence—if you do some work to look past the fantastic gains of speed and manic social grooming—you'll catch only glimpses of that earlier mentality. Lost absence flits from your gaze like the floaters on the eye's lens, which we sometimes apprehend but can never focus on. To sense the end of absence is to intuit only.

I can make my little changes now. I turn off the phone, I ignore the e-mail; I do seek out solitude. Not pathologically, but enough. It was just small changes, really. Those, and this larger one: the fact that I feel *awake* to the end of absence, now. It hurts a little more to be without it.

So I take these small steps up the trail, I come back to the green hill. That's the job I'm giving myself. Come back to the green hill, look around, look just here and just with my eyes, look alone. It's as though absence were a supernatural jewel that I dropped somewhere in the grass. It's that hidden—and that priceless.

Joseph Weizenbaum, the man who invented ELIZA, predicted in his 1976 book, *Computer Power and Human Reason*, that the computer would now "intrude itself into the very stuff out of which man builds his world." He believed that our computers were integral parts of our perception and being—that we truly are cyborgs. He foretold that ripping the computer tool from us would be as damaging to society as ripping out a lung from a body. But that can't be the whole story.

Each technology is born of a particular global context, rife with specific economic, political, and even doctrinal expectations. We need, as Neil Postman suggests, a "psychic distance from any technology" so that it always appears strange to us, "never inevitable, never natural."

Homeward bound. Here I stand on the bus, its progress shaking me a little in my place as I hang one-armed from the strap. And all around me, the young and not so young are banishing their boredom by pouring their attention into games like *Angry Birds* and *Jewel Quest* on their phones. The bus rattles around a corner and we all sway in unison, we bump into one another, but nobody looks up. An elderly woman, with perfect white hair, turns to look out the window and appears to disappear.

. . . . .

Jaron Lanier wrote that "one good test of whether an economy is humanistic or not is the plausibility of earning the ability to drop out of it for a while without incident or insult." This seems a good gauge to me. And I know that dropping out of our current information economy would indeed damage my livelihood, put me at odds with the "ordinary" lives of my peers. It's this fact of the hassle—the incorrectness of dropping off the grid—that solidifies my ambition to do it.

I decide that I *will* take that sabbatical from the future. For thirty days, I will return to something akin to the technological circumstances of my childhood. No Internet. No mobile phone. No Twitter or Facebook or text messages; no self-diagnosis of pneumonia on Mayoclinic.org. I alert all my editors, family members, and closest friends that they can phone me if they want to, but if I'm away from home, they'll have to leave a message because my phone is now duct-taped to a phone cord I found at Future Shop and that cord is, itself, duct-taped to the kitchen counter. And then I walk away.

. . . . .

MY ANALOG AUGUST

August 1

Every morning Kenny and I eat our cereal next to each other at the long wooden table, each facing our respective laptops. It's nice. We look at our blogs and collect necessary narratives for dispersal throughout the day with other happy informed citizens. I'll call

Kenny over to check out a trailer for the new *Hunger Games* and he'll pull me over to see a piece of animation from London's The Line studio. We dip our heads in the ocean together.

This morning K. went to his usual post and I sat at the kitchen table alone with my raisin bran. I blinked at the empty chair across from me and called to the next room: "You don't want to come have breakfast?"

"I *am* having breakfast."

"I mean with *me*."

"No, I'm okay." There's a video playing on repeat and K.'s cracking up.

Torture.

Feels like I just stepped off an incredibly fast ride and the sheer *s-l-o-w-n-e-s-s* of everything is freaking me out. Every five minutes my brain asks me to look up a fact or an image that it's lacking. What does Kate's baby look like, again? How many references to robots are there in Alan Turing's scientific papers? It feels insane to not be allowed to know. I have to let questions constantly slide away, unanswered.

Hello, 1987.

August 2

I thought I'd feel comfortable asking strangers for the time but, instead, have been forced to constantly buy things in order to check time on receipts. Then Kenny gave me a watch today. Very funny contraption. I feel like a man with a pipe.

August 3

Impulse to check e-mail continues unabated. Definite sense that I'm maiming my own career and have grown certain that several lucrative book/movie deals are expiring in my in-box.

The phone is, meanwhile, surprisingly easy to leave at home. I keep picking it up, though, on my return, expecting dozens of messages. In fact, only person to contact me in past 48 hours was a volunteer from a charity service called Big Brothers. (A sign?)

Went for leisurely cocktail at West with K. and Vince this eve, then home alone for viewing of *Pride & Prejudice* while they went out for Pride weekend beer-up. I was in bed by ten; have arrived at "recluse" stage faster than expected.

August 6

The instinct to check e-mail comes naturally each morning, insistent as the urge to shower, to put on the kettle. I feel unawake without messages, as though am wrapped in some cotton batting. Simultaneously: feel like a child who ran away from home and then was crushed to discover nobody noticed his disappearance.

August 8

I dream of e-mail. All night I crafted perfect missives to Barack Obama and Kirsten Dunst. Alas.

August 11

Stood in Chapters for half an hour reading a cover story in *Fast Company* by a man called Baratunde Thurston who disconnected from Internet for 25 days. Felt very smug reading it as Thurston was still texting and using Google Calendar; he even had a personal assistant log in every few days to make sure he didn't "miss anything urgent." Thurston writes that he experienced "an expansion of sensations and ideas" (vague) during his quasi sabbatical, which leaves me very excited about my true sabbatical as my more extreme disconnection will surely lead to a proper epiphany that surpasses his meager revelations.

August 14

No epiphany quite yet.

It is *still* hard. (Though not physically sick-making, anymore.)

Benjamin Franklin is helpful—he had this notion of "philosophical self-denial," which William Powers writes about:

> You have to see that there is more to be gained by resisting the impulse than giving in. Once you truly believe this, it's all downhill. What previously seemed a dreary, priggish way to live—denying oneself pleasure—suddenly becomes positive and even hedonistic.

Meanwhile, I spent two hours today looking up things in books I could have sourced online in thirty seconds. Perhaps the hedonism comes later.

August 15

Each morning I kiss K. good-bye and he goes off to work at his new studio gig; I remain at home with the breakfast dishes and try not to give in. I imagine K. interacting all day with other clever artists—he's storyboarding the new Seth Rogen flick and so, no doubt, lunches in chic Gastown rooms with the beautiful tribe, decked in Frank & Oak shirts and toting Hirschel bags.

Through his phone, K.'s in touch with a few people before breakfast, in fact. I hardly cared before, but now our early-morning, toothbrush-in-mouth conversations seem nastily pruned by the endless ping-ping-ping. It often happens that, even before K. has left the apartment, he's touched more lives than I will all day. I pad about the rooms with a book and pen, looking forward, pathetically, to the thrill of my Starbucks trip.

Working from home was far more bearable when e-mail and texts provided a soft, ambient sense of connection to the outside world. Technologies, I guess, support an attitude in which feelings only count when they are expressed; and this leaves me unwilling to believe my days really matter when I can't share them. It's no good to think of our experience as reducible to tweets and instant messages, but it's equally pointless to live an unshared life.

Dilemma.

August 19

Did a *Where's Waldo* at the café. Shocking bad sign.

August 21

On the unexpected pleasures of pamphlets, I could now write a treatise. Each day I await the mail carrier with a mortifying degree of suspense. Usually he arrives between 11 a.m. and 11:15, but today he did not arrive until half past noon. (The awareness of this transgression places me in the company of an over-starched Barbara Pym heroine.) Naturally, all news, all *content,* is now a precious alert from the wider world. I read "exciting offers" from credit card companies and think, "Yes, that *is* exciting"; I read newsletters from local politicians with unprecedented interest and today spent twenty minutes poring over a Pottery Barn catalog. Soon I'll be one of those people who stop to chat with petitioners at Broadway and Granville.

P.S. I now read *newspapers.*

August 22

We just can't handle solitude without a rich interior life. At first there was this bewildering, wind-swept void where my online world had been. Now, haltingly, I place other things in that void. A book. A walk through Shaughnessy to monitor the construction of various McMansions I have my eye on. But, of course, nothing—*nothing*—is as enthralling as the lovely, comforting, absence-destroying Internet. You can't really revert to a prior state of mind because (as Nicholas Carr points out) our brains may be changeable and plastic, but they aren't necessarily *elastic.* My online mind waits angrily for its food.

August 23

My tolerance toward interruption has plummeted. (Good sign? Bad sign?) During a chat at the pub, or on the seawall, my interlocutor will raise a finger (pressing an invisible hold button in the air between us) and answer an incoming text message with a sort of blithe assumption that my own attention will immediately flit somewhere else in the meantime. But, without my phone on hand, I simply stare into this white noise and wait.

The real annoyance, though, is not with conversation pauses; it's with the dullness of the conversations such fractures produce. A divided self is simply not a worthwhile thing to focus on.

So then I disengage—I'll start daydreaming or I'll study a mosquito bite—and we end up with a case of Compound Distraction.

August 24

Was at first distraught to find that everyone I informed about Analog August wanted to know what my epiphany had been. Surely, if I was going to all this trouble, I must be experiencing an inner transformation. Or perhaps my interrogators felt the exercise was pointless but assumed I would claim such a transformation to save face.

Have found myself a little desperate to make something up. The closest thing I can report, though, won't sound dramatic enough. It's just this: Behavior that seemed utterly normal on the 30th of July now looks compulsive and animalistic. Now when I see teenage girls burrowed into their phones on the sidewalk I think of monkeys picking lice out of each other's hair.

August 25

In the 17th century, newspaper readers in coffeehouses were thought to be antisocial and indulging in a "sullen silence." Today they're a charming part of the mise-en-scène. Time settles everything. One day soon we'll contentedly discuss dreams that appeared to us as bright blue bubbles of text.

My day's activities included: a visit to the bank to pay a bill; sending a printed chapter of my book to Matthew in Ottawa; Mailbox (11:45!); 40 minutes ogling Shaughnessy mansions; 30 minutes reading Coupland's riff on McLuhan's *The Medium Is the Message*.

But nothing feels productive (i.e., nothing makes me money).

Increasingly disturbed by how hamstrung my work-life is without Internet. I can't take on new projects, or even invoice for old ones. I sweep and tidy my desktop instead. My free time is capacious. Found myself disappointed when I checked my toenails and saw it wasn't time to clip them yet.

August 26

Bertrand Russell says in *Conquest of Happiness* that the ability to fill leisure time intelligently is the last product of civilization. I guess I thought I'd start filling my own free hours more intelligently once I cut out the cat videos and Bret Easton Ellis tweets. But no.

I appear to be as much of a moron offline as on. The real difference is that my unintelligent behavior is much more painfully obvious now. Which is something to hold on to, if not to cherish.

August 27

I wanted to remember the absences that online life had replaced with constant content, constant connection. I've remembered what it is to be free in the world, free from the obliterating demands of five hundred "contacts." But, of all the absences I've remembered, there's one that is the greatest, the most encompassing—that is solitude.

And yet, of this absence, a little goes a long way. 1987, it turns out, makes for a crushingly lonely vacation. Still, if solitude feels painful it's only because we don't know how to be alone.

August 28

Friends who've done the West Coast Trail talk with glassy eyes about the White Spot burgers and 24-ounce Cokes that get downed on the ferry ride home. The religious consumption of that long-denied high-fructose injection. I've been thinking about what I'm going to eat first—digitally speaking—when I go back online.

E-mail, obviously. I fantasize with a starved man's mind about sitting down at the laptop with notepad at the ready, a cup of piping coffee . . . how I'll just let it *run* over me, a joyful sabotaging of the calm mediocrity I've been engineering this past month.

August 29

It *is* possible to abstain. To know full well the hefty glamour of the world's shining face and then, for a time, step away.

But exactly what part of me I'd be abstaining from wasn't clear before I tried this. How large a portion of my life was enmeshed so thoroughly in online technologies that it could not be extricated. Social life stumbles forward at half-speed, perhaps. But work grinds to a halt. In the entire month, only *one* work-related phone-call. The rest of my peers and editors, on receiving my bounce-back alert stating that I'm not online, appear to have written me off for dead. How much money have I lost? And how many chances?

September 1

Game over. But we're on an island. It'd be sacrilege to binge on e-mail here. Now that it's come down to it, waiting a few more days doesn't feel like anything at all.

September 3

Back home from the Gulf Islands. Last night K. and I fought.

After dinner I glanced around like I was about to commit a crime and cracked my laptop, freed its wireless settings, dove into the 264 buzzing e-mails that were waiting for me, all aglow. This, naturally, meant ignoring K. for the course of the evening. He'd ask what I was looking at and I'd mutter one-word answers without looking away from the screen. His monk-like boyfriend— who tutted at the distractions of others—had blipped out of existence.

And what a sweet ride, to slice through that stack of missives! Of the 264 messages, 100 were easily junked. A further hundred required only single-sentence replies, which I issued with a rat-tat-tat military efficiency. And *such* efficiency! Such quick arrows of accomplishment! Meanwhile, K. grew increasingly annoyed at my happy-robot distance. I left the in-box at 11 p.m., with about 60 thought-requiring messages left for me to tackle in the morning; sated, I trotted off to bed. It wasn't until then, as I laid myself down to sleep, that I floated back to my surroundings and became aware of K.'s anger, aware that I'd utterly botched my first day back online.

Coupland warned me not to expect an epiphany from all this. An epiphany? Maybe no. But it's the break itself that's the thing. It's the break—that is, the questioning—that snaps us out of the spell, that can convince us it was a spell in the first place.

Perhaps, despite the dullness, despite the cotton-stuffed torture that goes along with 31 days of disconnection (the very opposite of epiphany, of gaining access to some new understanding), I have learned something after all. That I am so irrevocably, damnably, utterly wired to the promise of connection that I have to constantly, every hour of every day, choose *which* connections matter in a given moment. I'm not going to fast away the distracted parts of my brain with a month-long Internet sabbatical; if I'm going to live intelligently *in* the world, I'll have to do it every hour of my life. How exhausting, I thought to myself, as these conditions dawned on me in the shower this morning. How very exhausting. Yet how very worth it.

· · · · ·

There's this idea that keeps getting whispered through history. It was Thoreau who first suggested it to me, the idea that we aren't lonely because we are alone; we are lonely because we have failed in our solitude. Thoreau was never seeking out loneliness, after all. He went to the woods *because* of his loneliness; he went into the woods to enjoy the company of his bare self. Here was a twenty-eight-year-old Harvard-educated man who walked out of town with a borrowed ax and, using native lumber and scrap wood, built himself a twelve-by-fifteen-foot cabin to live in; his nearest neighbor was a mile away. He dug a root cellar in the soil. He planted a bean field. He had no job, but he read and wrote and watched the woods around him. He gave himself two full years there to "follow the bent of my genius." As surely as the Internet burrows pathways into our neural network, Thoreau wore a pathway from his hut to Walden Pond. He seemed to prefigure our understanding of neuroplasticity when he wrote: "The surface of the earth is soft and impressible by the feet of men; and so with the paths which the mind travels."

But which paths did Thoreau think we should follow? What exactly was Thoreau's idea of good solitude? I returned to my own copy of *Walden*. Rereading that distillation of quiet wisdom again, I was struck by one well-trotted line:

> I went to the woods because I wished to live deliberately,
> to front only the essential facts of life, and see if I could
> not learn what it had to teach, and not, when I came to
> die, discover that I had not lived.

But it's the sentence that follows that adage, a less famous line, that I want to unpack here. Thoreau goes on to say, "I did not wish to live what was not life, living is so dear." *I did not wish to live what was not life.* There are two ambitious assumptions being made here. The first assumption is that the bulk of the buying and selling and *managing* that makes up the everyman's daily existence can be set to one side and counted as "not life."[21] The second assumption Thoreau makes is that once we discern what is "real life" and what is not, we can then cut away the fat. His book is the knife he offers.

Walden is nothing so clear-cut and encouraging as the

21. More than a century later, Thoreau's words seem reflected in the work of poet Anne Carson: "When I think of you reading this I do not want you to be taken captive, separated by a wire mesh lined with glass from your life itself, like some Elektra."

self-help guidebooks we now hoist to the best-seller branches of Amazon charts. It means, rather, to outline a mental crisis and then leave each reader to step into that frame of reference should he or she choose. I wonder if, one day, *Walden* will be carried around on the tablets of the young as a kind of security blanket to ward off the crush of connectivity they were born into. Perhaps it will deliver the same intense meaning for those youths as *The Sorrows of Young Werther* once did for eighteenth-century German youths. A totem for a new Romanticism. Perhaps, instead of taking Grand Tours of Europe, future youths will embark on a tour of Solitude. A Grand Absence. Might they roam through the backcountry of their own lives? (Probably not.)

I've asked myself many times, in the course of my research for this book: What Would Thoreau Do? Would he, rather than shut himself in a cramped hut for a couple of years, refuse to pick up a phone for as long a stretch? Would he murder his social media avatars? Our twenty-first-century Thoreau would have difficulty discerning the limits of his experiment: Is banking permissible, since it's so utterly reliant upon electronic transactions? Where would he draw the line? Arguments could be made against any aspect of life, since none is untouched by the Internet's influence.

Thoreau was a latter-day Spartan, but also a deeply prudent man, which makes it difficult to know how far he'd take things today. Still, we know that even Thoreau—even in the midst of his two years at Walden Pond—was no absolutist. He had his clothes mended by folk in the nearby village. He purchased bits of pork and handfuls of salt, to complement the beans and turnips he grew for himself. Rice, which he could not grow, was a major staple of his diet. I don't think the goal was ever to cut himself off from society—far from it. The goal was to steer himself into crowds only when and how he saw fit. To not be drowned by "what was not life." To limit the number of moments that brought him into the society of other men and women and thus to make them more meaningful. Later in his book, we see again that his motives are a lust for life, not a fear of it: "I did not wish to take a cabin passage, but rather to go before the mast and on the deck of the world, for there I could best see the moonlight amid the mountains. I do not wish to go below now."

Just as Thoreau never pretended that cutting out society entirely was an option—and never, as a humane person, wanted to be entirely removed—we shouldn't pretend that deleting the Internet, undoing the online universe, is an option for us. Why would we, after all, want to delete, undo, something that came from us? It bears repeating: Technology is neither good nor evil. The most we can say about it is this: *It has come.* Casting judgments on the technologies themselves is like casting judgment on a bowl of tapioca pudding. We can only judge, only really profit from judging, the decisions we each make in our interactions *with* those technologies. How shall we live now? How will you?

More than 150 years ago, Thoreau worried about you and the future you inhabit. As he sat in his cabin, he could hear whistles and rumbles along the Fitchburg Railroad, which ran nearby. "The whistle of the locomotive penetrates my woods . . . informing me that many restless city merchants are arriving within the circle of the town." Thoreau mentions that doing things "railroad fashion" (meaning quickly, efficiently) has become a byword and he writes about the implacable *sureness* of the new iron technology as it barrels forward, blasting its whistle. "And it is worth the while to be warned so often and so sincerely by any power to get off its track. There is no stopping to read the riot act, no firing over the heads of the mob, in this case. We have constructed a fate . . . that never turns aside."

. . . . .

The steam-powered locomotive (which arrived at the front end of the nineteenth century) may have been a sign of that dangerous fate for Thoreau, but only a few generations later, train travel had already become a symbol of an idyllic, slower past. We see that in Glenn Gould's radio documentary "The Idea of North" (part of his *Solitude Trilogy*). The work takes place (if anywhere) on a train trundling along 1,015 miles of track between Winnipeg and Fort Churchill in Canada's barren north. Why *do* people go north into so much nothing? Gould wanted to know. So he took the train himself and struck up a conversation in the dining car with a surveyor named Wally, who became a sort of narrator for the piece. Along with Wally's voice, we get a small chorus of others, men and women drawn to the supposed wasteland miles and miles above Canada's "habitable" region, whose voices rise and fall like instruments in a chamber group, now overlapping, now speaking solo, to create an impressionistic meaning out of multiple associated viewpoints. Gould found that the folk heading north were motivated not really by the supposed desire to escape humanity, but rather by the impulse to embrace the very human parts of our lives that can be grasped only from within a certain solitude. In one television interview, Gould said that the people on that northbound train had something to find out about themselves: "They wanted to make inquiries about themselves."

Gould had a theory that for every hour a person spends in the company of others, the sane person ought to spend a certain (larger) number of hours on his or her own (he didn't know exactly how many hours that'd be, but he figured it was "a substantial ratio"). He valued communication but wanted it in particular doses, and he certainly wanted it on his own terms. Despite this quasi-hermit attitude, his few friends were harassed regularly by charming, infuriatingly long, excited phone calls. His fans were often disappointed by concert cancellations—until he stopped giving concerts entirely in 1964. He had decided to devote his practice entirely to electronic media and focused his career on recordings (in his way, Gould was reflecting the ideas in McLuhan's *The Gutenberg Galaxy*, which had been published just two years earlier).

The train to Fort Churchill is still making its slog for those who choose to disappear into the tundra. About twenty-three thousand passengers—heading into what absence?—take that train each year.

I'm on another train at present, writing these lines in a car of *The Canadian* at a pace that Thoreau would have called racing, I call pleasantly rolling, and my children will consider glacial. We're making our way through the Rocky Mountains, far from the tendrils of Internet signal. My fellow travelers and I resign ourselves to conversation with one another, but when we pass through a town, one will leap up in his sweatpants and hold his cell phone aloft: "Got a signal!" And then the carful will dig out their own phones and rapidly download e-mails or call up mapping apps to pin themselves on a digital landscape. The moment is short-lived, though. In a minute or two we've slipped, once more, into the obscuring wilderness, flanked by the hush of Canadian pine forests.

· · · · ·

Can we ever recall our former selves in a lasting way? Can we truly remember absence? Aren't some things gone forever?

We know that the spread of writing, in Harold Innis's words, "checked the growth of myth and made the Greeks skeptical of their gods." We know that "the immortal inconclusiveness of Plato was no longer possible" once the technology of writing wiped away a certain mystery. Some sensibilities may require a particular technological environment. And just as oral culture could then be understood only through the lens of writing, the scribal culture that followed would one day be viewed, says Elizabeth Eisenstein, "through a veil of print." Earlier viewpoints become clouded to future generations. How can we ever see the world as they did when we look through such different lenses? We have no real comprehension of the oral traditions that the written word wiped out or the scribal tradition that the printing press deleted. We cannot entirely know what we lost. So how will our children know what is disappearing now? Another veil is being drawn; it may come to pass that pre-Internet culture will be viewed only through a baffling screen beaded with 1s and 0s.

. . . . .

The value of absence is always an intangible thing, whether that absence is a memory or a current reality. Yet, in quiet ways, we get our hints.

Anthony Storr, writing about poetic inspiration, notes that "by far the greater number of new ideas occur during a state of reverie, intermediate between waking and sleeping." My favorite creative personalities always seem to have just returned from some isolating tower or other. I wonder, for example, if the shocking "jazz" elements that cropped up in Beethoven's later years were in fact thanks to his deafness. Did his auditory absence free him from preconceived notions? We need such absences in order to think and see for ourselves. Indeed, the kinds of thoughts that present themselves in our emptiest moments—the moments when we stare out the train's windows or hover on a lawn to monitor the sky—are the only thoughts that can deliver a strange new understanding. Such understandings, such experiences, cannot be programmed or puzzled out, but must be felt in the bracing air of absence. We have decades of studies showing that our psychological state, too, responds well to a little solitude. Rural settings enhance mental faculties and check the aggressive, neurotic tendencies we foster when we never get out on our own. The spaces in our lives that technologies filled in were never such barren places after all. Those spaces were where we stored our magic, our hope, and the longing that drove our striving souls.

Seneca tells us that "men's greatest achievements are the products of their seclusion." Yet most of us, most of the time, are living not in seclusion, but in a state of "restless idleness," flitting from one stimulating conversation or curiosity to the next, then and now. Flitting may be too kind. Elsewhere, Seneca refers to "the restless energy of a hunted mind." Ultimately, he argues for balance and for decisive choices:

> It is, however, necessary to combine the two things, solitude and the crowd, and to have recourse to them alternately: the former will make us long for people, the latter for ourselves, and the one will be a cure for the other: our distaste for the crowd will be cured by solitude, our boredom with solitude by the crowd.

Seneca, like Thoreau and like Gould, is far from a misanthrope. He desires that our connections be more valued, more imbued with meaning, more purposeful. And that we not be terrified of a little time with our fascinating selves.

Some are already working toward the preservation of absence. There's the Sloth Club in Japan, which promotes the "slow life movement" and runs the often candlelit Café Slow in Tokyo. Or the Long Now Foundation in the United States, which designed (and is currently building inside a mountain in western Texas) a clock that will run for ten thousand years, defying our obsession with speedy gains. There are still monasteries, nunneries, and Buddhist retreats. Software engineers are delivering programs like Freedom, Anti-Social, and Pomodoro, all designed to shield you from a maelstrom of computer-derived distraction. And there are authors like Susan Cain, writing books such as *Quiet* in order to meditate on "the power of introverts in a world that can't stop talking."

But these, of course, are the exceptions. And the desire to hold on to absence, to throw cold water on the spiraling apprehension of the busy mind, may be a fleeting one in the course of human events. The historian of ideas Noga Arikha positions herself the same way I position myself, as one "lucky enough to come from somewhere else, from a time when information was not digitized." She feels it's that outsider status—our status as the last of the daydreamers—that gives us the chance to use the Internet and all digital media with a measure of wisdom. It's a fantastic position, truly, to be in—we digital immigrants will be extinct in half a century and, with us, the balancing act that Arikha wrote of:

> I waver . . . at times gratefully dependent on this marvel, at times horrified at what this dependence signifies . . . the reduction of three-dimensionality to that flat screen. . . . Where has slowness gone, and tranquility, solitude, quiet? The world I took for granted as a child, and which my childhood books beautifully represented, jerks with the brand-new world of artificial glare . . . faster, louder, unrelated to nature.

I think Arikha, like all people alive in this moment, is engaged in an act of massive translation. We are the few translators of Before and After. It's a privileged thing to be a translator, but not an easy thing. Marshall McLuhan foretold our discomfort:

> Those who experience the first onset of a new technology, whether it be alphabet or radio, respond most emphatically because the new sense ratios set up at once by the technological dilation of eye or ear, present men with a surprising new world. . . . But the real revolution is in this later and prolonged phase of "adjustment" of all personal and social life to the new model of perception set up by the new technology.

How long will our phase of adjustment last? Another twenty years, another fifty? Will readers of these words, even ten years from now, have kept in mind the adjustment that came before? Will they recognize that adjustments in our attitudes reflect more fundamental changes? And what pains, discomforts, and revolutions of *yours,* dear future reader, will be forgotten by those who follow? What curious and new things will become inevitable and natural to others? What bright and eager lives will you call delusionary?

. . . . .

Absence isn't going to return to us easily. Just as we decide to limit our intake of the sugars and fats that we're designed to hoard, we now must decide to sometimes keep at bay the connectivity we're hardwired to adore. We must remain as critical of technological progress as we are desirous of it. And we must make these decisions not because we dislike the things we could connect to, but precisely because they're so crucial to our survival.

Every technology will alienate you from some part of your life. That is its job. *Your* job is to notice. First notice the difference. And then, every time, choose.

EPILOGUE
What Comes Across, What Stays Behind

"THE end of absence" is a disobliging subject—precisely because it looks, to the casual eye, like a lovely collection of gains. What's more, once an absence is ended, we can hardly remember what use it had to begin with. Indeed, why complain at all? Bemoaning the end of an absence is, it seems, the duty of Luddites and cranks. Which is to say, we brush off those who eulogize such losses.

Besides, maybe the real eulogy was delivered a long time ago. We all like to think we're living on the brink of the future, that this is the pivot point, but wasn't our pace of life largely settled in the nineteenth century? In the shuttering of the Arts and Crafts movement and the final silencing of the bleeding Romantic poets, we find the last stand of some pre-modern sensibility. The boldest of these stands was made by those famous resisters— the Luddites (they suffered the firmest stamping out, too).

I've been called a "Luddite" a few times while working on this book. It always surprised me, because my approach is hardly a call to arms. Part of me is very ready to let the Giant Robot in the Sky take care of me. The breezy availability of new cloud technologies is as comforting and omnipresent as a god in the heavens. It's only a small and stubborn part of me that resists and worries about the end of daydreaming and all that.

But the "Luddite" tag left me wondering . . . who were the Luddites, really? It turns out that the original nineteenth-century Luddites were hardly "Luddites" in our contemporary sense at all. We think of such people as being rabidly and unthinkingly anti-technology. But in fact the Luddites of Nottingham, and Lancashire, and Yorkshire—the textile workers who attacked the "power loom" in 1811 and beyond—were socialist revolution-aries, a group of workers who fought against crippling pay cuts, child labor, and changes to laws that had protected their liveli-hoods. They were fighting not *against* technology, but *for* fair treatment at the hands of a manufacturing elite. As Neil Postman has it: "The historical Luddites were neither childish nor naïve. They were people trying desperately to preserve whatever rights, privileges, laws, and customs had given them justice in the older world-view." They were not anti-tech; they were pro-people. These so-called reactionaries also prefigured the modern union ethic, which would safeguard the rights and lives of so many.

· · · · ·

What, then, should we ask of ourselves? I don't think attacking Tumblr in a neo-Luddite revolution would do much good. But what are our responsibilities?

This book is a meditation more than a prescription. There are no ten easy steps to living a healthy digital life; there is no totalizing theory, no maxim, with which we can armor our-selves. Nor is digital abstinence the answer, absolute refusal be-ing just another kind of dependence, after all.

Easy fixes are for easy problems. And what do real problems, big problems, call for? Experimentation and play. So here's a pseudoprescription: Give yourself permission to go without some weekend—without any of the screens you look at when you're bored. (Yes, you'll feel anxious, at loose ends, but then what?) Ask yourself what might come from all those silences you've been filling up. What if you told your five-year-old the Internet was closed for Christmas vacation? What if you told yourself that?

Experiment. Live a little. And remember that fear of absence is the surest sign that absence is direly needed.

· · · · ·

It's in moments of mass change—as witnessed by the Luddites—that our most constant qualities appear. I'm with Ezra Pound, who felt moments of translation are always moments of clarity: It's in moments of translation that we learn what's indelible about us. We see what cannot pass forward into the new language, the new life, but we also see what things remain.

Here's one indestructible thing:

Think of Chunyun, the period of travel in China leading up to the Lunar New Year. Over the course of two weeks, the world's largest annual human migration takes place, with hundreds of millions of migrant workers and students returning home to be with their families, stretching the limits of rail systems (packed with citizens who cannot afford airfare). This is a country more connected to the Internet than any other, and it is also the site of humanity's single largest expression of the basic drive to connect in person, its citizens putting up with slow and cumbersome travel in order to arrive at a more authentic bond.

Slower, more rare possibilities remain there, beneath the maelstrom of digital life. And the two kinds of connection—fast and slow, constant and rare—can even work together:

This summer, my brother and sister-in-law flew to Melbourne, Australia, to introduce their one-year-old boy, Levi, to his maternal grandmother. My nephew had seen his grandma only through weekly video chats online, knew her only as a cheerful image on a computer's screen. Yet in Melbourne Airport—after twenty-three exhausting hours of travel—Levi (a shy infant, skeptical of strangers) held out his arms to his grandmother the moment he saw her and hugged her around the neck as though to say, "Oh, *there* you are!"

GLOSSARY

THE end of absence is enigmatic; to talk about it, we need new words.

ANNOTATION DEPENDENCE

The contention that everything ought to be gilded in supporting text. *Looking up from the Google Map, Brady was discomfited to find himself in a baffling network of poorly labeled streets.*

AVATAR CRUSH

The realization that someone's online persona is infinitely preferable to his or her flesh-and-blood self. *Sarah was hilarious in text form, but I only had an avatar crush. In person she smelled like boiled eggs.*

BETAPHOBIA

The fear of missing out on the first wave of a new technology. *Carlos got a serious hit of betaphobia when he saw her robotic dog ambling over to meet them.*

CLOUD FAITH

The assumption that algorithms and crowdsourced data will invariably derive more meaningful outcomes. *Long ago, Derek had decided to choose movies based on cloud faith.*

COMPOUND DISTRACTION

The experience of one person's distraction compounding another's. *Julie kept texting while I was talking about my cat, so I started texting, too.* Exists in two varietals: "Limited compound distraction" refers to a moment of positive feedback (*Bailey kept texting while I was telling him about the exam, so I started tweeting about it instead*), whereas "assumed compound distraction" refers to a predetermined atmosphere of distraction wherein sustained, meaningful interaction feels awkward and unwelcome (*Harry and Bryce mumbled to each other about Iran while scrolling through the news on their respective phones*).

CONDITION CREEP

The degree to which each generation loosens its privacy settings and becomes more at ease with purveyors of big data. Typified by the automatic acceptance of unread "terms and conditions." *Jonah's dad noted a bit of condition creep when he saw the links to homemade porn on his son's Twitter feed.*

DÉJÀ ZEITGEIST

The sense that all content is now merely a revision of content from earlier decades. *Why didn't I think of that* Archie *satire?*

DERIVAPHILIA

The love of derivative content over original content. *Did you see the* Dr. Who *T-shirt Liam made? Amazing.*

DISCONNECTION RAGE

A sudden and unaccountably fierce meltdown brought on by five minutes of lost access to the Internet. *Susan bawled out the harried barista when the café's Wi-Fi signal faltered.*

FLASH CARD CONFESSIONAL

A genre of video in which the creator—typically a teenage female—confesses private trauma through a series of flash cards bearing Sharpie text. *The whole school saw her flash card confessional, so now she was a loser and an attention whore, too.*

GOING WALDEN

The often ill-conceived decision to live without connective technologies for a period of time in order to cleanse the spirit. *"While we're in Bali," said Harry, "what if we went totally Walden?"*

LENS AMNESIA

The experience of forgetting one is viewing reality through a particular technological lens. *George was shocked to discover that Rebecca had blurred out an unfortunate mole constellation in her profile photos.*

MEGAPPROVAL

The act of boosting something online in as many arenas as possible, often through passive "like" systems on Facebook and such. *It wasn't enough to just buy the new Death Cab for Cutie album, Tomer opened his laptop and started megapproving it.*

MICRO-DEATH

The state of waiting for a technology to complete an internal process, of being put on hold by a computer. *Julie's mouth dropped open an inch each time her tablet loaded a page.*

MINIGEN

A distinct group of people born within five years of one another. *At the party, all the kids a minigen younger than me were obsessed with memes I'd never heard of.*

OVERSPIRE

The experience of too much inspiration, resulting in no further gains in creativity. *Over the weekend I watched a dozen TED Talks in a row and got this vaguely overspired feeling.*

PHONE BURROW

The act of becoming dead to the world while pouring all attention into a phone. (Often more obvious in public spaces.) *She froze in the intersection, dove into full phone burrow, and let her umbrella drop to the pavement.*

PHONE DODGE

The act of compulsively checking one's phone in an awkward situation. *Susan's friends weren't at the bar yet, so she pulled a phone dodge and became fascinated by her Pinterest feed.*

PHONE LEASH

The limit from home that one can travel without a phone before anxiety kicks in. *He got two blocks down the street before his phone leash whipped him around.*

SLOWNET

Programs that allow users to limit their access to online content. *Mariko kept on getting sucked into Katy Perry videos, so she jacked up her slownet settings.*

STACCATO LOVE

A relationship maintained by short and detached bursts of intensely affectionate messaging. *Just one of Christina's staccato love messages could keep him going for a week: OMG U R soooooooooo cute!!! ;-)*

STRADDLE GENERATION

Neither digital natives nor wholly digital immigrants: They were born in the 1980s and will be the last people to remember life without the Internet. *After she got text-dumped, Stacey was determined to date only straddle gen guys. "They're so romantic!"*

SUPER-SANCTION

The act of granting worth or authenticity to something by upping its digital presence. For example, broadcasting images of the food one is about to consume. (Related to an Enlightenment bias that presumes making information available is akin to making it valuable.) *Before tucking in, the men gave their steaks a super-sanction on Instagram.*

TANDEM TALK

The act of cruising Google in tandem with a phone conversation in order to source info or anecdotes and bolster one's own ideas. *I thought Derek knew a lot about water bears, but it turned out he was just tandem talking.*

TECH DILATION

An increased commitment to visual information, as encouraged by certain technologies. *Tom's eyes were bugged out with tech dilation after burrowing into his phone for twenty minutes.*

TECHAPROPISM

The appropriation of computer terminology to describe real-life experiences. *Nick walked into the party and muttered to his girlfriend, "None of your preferred networks are available."*

UNICORN

A person with no online presence who thus boasts a ghostly or mythical quality when he or she shows up in person. *Clay's Facebook sabbatical lent him a unicorn quality and upped his cachet at grad parties.*

UNMEMBER

To off-load a memory from brain to computer. *It was such a relief to unmember Dai's boyfriend's name.*

WAGGING THE CROWD

Purposeful manipulation of ratings on crowd-based voting systems like Yelp. *Jim's restaurant was failing, so he hired a click farm in India to wag the crowd.*

ACKNOWLEDGMENTS

MANY people, wittingly or no, have helped bring this book together. I want to thank first Linda Jimi, who allowed an amazing chapter of her life to become my prologue. For taking the time to explain their research and ideas to me, huge thanks go to Lewis Altfest, Matt Atchity, Noel Biderman, Susan Blackmore, Ken Boesem, Peter Bregman, Morris Chapdelaine, Douglas Coupland, Nelson Cowan, Dave Craven, Dennis Danielson, Karthik Dinakar, Sidney D'Mello, Paul Eastwick, Markus Frind, Douglas Gentile, James Heilman, Dan Hobbins, Alberto Manguel, Andrew Ng, Heather O'Brien, Elias Roman, Gary Small, Carol Todd, and Jonathan Wegener.

This book would not exist without the vision of my superb agent, Anne McDermid, whose team I'm also indebted to. Editors in two offices were endlessly patient with a first-time author and made this book much, much better: Thanks to Jennifer Lambert at HarperCollins and to Maria Gagliano and Rachel Moore at Current. Thanks also to Brooke Carey, who believed in this project early on.

Early research was supported by assignments from two excellent editors: Rachel Giese at *Walrus* magazine and John Burns at *Vancouver* magazine.

For expansive talks and critical readings, I'm indebted to my friends Ed Bergman, Tyee Bridge, Anne Casselman, Kerry Gold, Charles Montgomery, Matthew Pearson, Michael Scott, Paul Siggers, Elsa Wyllie, and Bryson Young. For research assistance, great thanks go to Kathleen Golner. And for their constant encouragement (and so many lessons on storytelling), I'm raising a glass of Joie to the editors and art directors—past and present—at the hallowed halls of TC Media.

To the Harris and Park families, none of whom believed me when I told them how long it takes to write a book, huge thanks for the constant love and kindness. Thanks especially to my parents—Bob and Marilyn.

Lady B., my ideal reader and blindest supporter: I'm in your debt for tea, sympathy, and constant loafs.

Kenny, my partner and best friend: You made this book possible through your unwavering, unwarranted kindness and support. Love you.

Kafka tells us that "one can never be alone enough when one writes." And I agree that moments of absence are necessary. But those stretches of solitude teach us to be more grateful for the just-as-necessary connections; the big journey of writing a book is neither envisioned nor completed in isolation.

NOTES

Prologue: This Can Show You Everything

1 *The settlement called Batu Lima:* Linda Jimi, interview with author, January 17, 2013. (The town in question is Kampung Kibbas.)

1 *One daughter:* Linda Jimi, interview with and e-mail message to author, January 17, 2013.

Part I: Gathering

5 *"We think we have discovered":* Maurice Maeterlinck, "La morale mystique," in *The Treasure of the Humble*, trans. Alfred Sutro (New York: Dodd, Mead & Co., 1903), 61–62.

Chapter I: This Kills That

7 *"Technology is neither good nor bad":* Melvin Kranzberg, "Technology and History: 'Kranzberg's Laws,'" *Technology and Culture* 27, no. 3 (1986): 544–60.

7 *a kind of foundational myth:* I'm using the broader sense of "myth" here, as defined by Roland Barthes in his 1957 book *Mythologies* (Paris: Editions du Seuil, 1957).

10 *"once people get used":* Gary Small and Gigi Vorgan, *iBrain: Surviving the Technological Alteration of the Modern Mind* (New York: HarperCollins, 2008), 18.

10 *"In the short run":* Ibid., 19.

13 *the printing machine itself:* Stephan Füssel, "Gutenberg and Today's Media Change," *Publishing Research Quarterly* 16, no. 4 (Winter 2001): 3–10.

14 *"a new medium is never":* Marshall McLuhan, *Understanding Media: The Extensions of Man* (Berkeley, Calif.: Gingko Press, 2003), 237.

16 *"I can only describe it personally":* Alberto Manguel, interview with author, April 29, 2013.

17 *"faucet of foolishness"*: Jean Cocteau, *Past Tense: The Cocteau Diaries* (New York: Harcourt Brace Jovanovich, 1988), 75.

17 *"every time someone switches it on"*: Groucho Marx, *Groucho Marx and Other Short Stories and Tall Tales: Selected Writings of Groucho Marx* (New York: Faber & Faber, 1993), xxix.

17 *"they can only give you answers"*: William Fifield, "Pablo Picasso: A Composite Interview," *Paris Review* 32 (Summer–Fall 1964): 62.

19 *we "liked" 4.5 billion items*: "Facebook's Growth in the Past Year," Facebook, accessed January 17, 2014, https://www.facebook.com/photo.php?fbid=10151908376831729&set=a.10151908376636729.1073741825.20531316728&type=1&theater.

19 *one hundred hours of video*: "Statistics," YouTube, accessed January 17, 2014, http://www.youtube.com/yt/press/statistics.html.

19 *637 photos to Instagram*: "Press Page," Instagram, accessed January 17, 2014, http://instagram.com/press/#.

19 *40 percent of all people*: "The World in 2013," *ICT Facts and Figures,* International Telecommunication Union, accessed January 17, 2014, http://www.itu.int/en/ITU-D/Statistics/Documents/facts/ICTFactsFigures2013-e.pdf.

19 *Social media trains our behavior:* Jeff Bullas published reports from the Global Web Index in "12 Awesome Social Media Facts and Statistics for 2013," accessed January 17, 2014, http://www.jeffbullas.com/2013/09/20/12-awesome-social-media-facts-and-statistics-for-2013/.

19 *93 percent of college students:* Merry J. Sleigh, Aimee W. Smith, and Jason Laboe, "Professors' Facebook Content Affects Students' Perceptions and Expectations," *Cyberpsychology, Behavior, and Social Networking* 16, no. 7 (2013): 489–96.

19 *In Malaysia:* Lim Yung-Hui, "Facebook in Asia," Forbes.com, accessed January 6, 2014, http://www.forbes.com/sites/limyunghui/2012/07/16/facebook-in-asia-growth-deceleration-continues-latest-stats/.

19 *Americans spent 520 billion:* "State of the Media: The Social Media Report 2012," Nielsen Company, accessed January 7, 2014, http://www.nielsen.com/content/dam/corporate/us/en/reports-downloads/2012-Reports/The-Social-Media-Report-2012.pdf.

20 *"A car or a plane enabled you":* Susan Greenfield, "Are We Becoming Cyborgs?," *New York Times,* November 30, 2012, http://

www.nytimes.com/2012/11/30/opinion/global/maria-popova-evgeny-morozov-susan-greenfield-are-we-becoming-cyborgs.html?_r=0.

21 *"the great handwriting of the human race"*: Victor Hugo, *Notre-Dame de Paris* (New York: Thomas Y. Crowell, 1888), 194.

22 *"Not till we are lost"*: Henry David Thoreau, *Walden* (New York: Everyman's Library, 1992), 153.

23 *According to research by Nielsen:* "New Mobile Obsession U.S. Teens Triple Data Usage," Nielsen Company, accessed January 6, 2014, http://www.nielsen.com/us/en/newswire/2011/new-mobile-obsession-u-s-teens-triple-data-usage.html.

Chapter 2: Kids These Days

25 *"Human brains are exquisitely evolved"*: Susan Greenfield, "Are We Becoming Cyborgs?," *New York Times*, November 30, 2012.

27 *As early as 2010:* "Generation M2: Media in the Lives of 8- to 18-Year-Olds," Kaiser Family Foundation, accessed January 7, 2014, http://www.kff.org/entmedia/mh012010pkg.cfm.

27 *Of course those youths, expert multitaskers:* Ibid.

28 *764 text messages each month:* "The Mobile Consumer: A Global Snapshot," Nielsen Company, accessed January 7, 2014, http://www.nielsen.com/content/dam/corporate/us/en/reports-downloads/2013%20Reports/Mobile-Consumer-Report-2013.pdf.

30 *"It may become what we expect"*: Sherry Turkle, *Alone Together: Why We Expect More from Technology and Less from Each Other* (New York: Basic Books, 2012), 295.

30 *A University of Michigan metastudy:* "Empathy: College Students Don't Have as Much as They Used To," University of Michigan News, accessed January 7, 2014, http://ns.umich.edu/new/releases/7724.

30 *increased levels of narcissism:* Jean M. Twenge, "The Evidence for Generation Me and Against Generation We," *Emerging Adulthood* 1, no. 1 (2013): 11–16.

31 *Radio took thirty-eight years:* Jay N. Giedd, "The Digital Revolution and Adolescent Brain Evolution," *Journal of Adolescent Health* 51, no. 2 (2012): 101–5.

31 *6.8 billion cell phone subscriptions:* "The World in 2013," *ICT Facts and Figures,* International Telecommunication Union.

31 *a sobering 99 percent saturation:* "The Mobile Consumer Report," Nielsen Company, accessed January 7, 2014, http://www.nielsen.com/us/en/reports/2013/mobile-consumer-report-february-2013.html.

31 *in China . . . a committed 6 percent:* Ibid.

32 *"O most ingenious Theuth":* Plato, *The Essential Plato* (New York: Quality Paperback Book Club, 1999), 844–45.

33 *The Florentine book merchant:* Elizabeth L. Eisenstein, *The Printing Revolution in Early Modern Europe,* 2nd ed. (New York: Cambridge University Press, 2005), 48.

34 *"Cortical areas that once":* John Brockman, ed., *Is the Internet Changing the Way You Think?: The Net's Impact on Our Minds and Future* (New York: Harper Perennial, 2011), 271.

34 *"For the most obvious character of print":* Marshall McLuhan, *The Gutenberg Galaxy* (Toronto: University of Toronto Press, 1962), 40.

34 *"The eye speeded up":* Ibid., 50.

34 *"shrill and expansive individualism":* Ibid., 18.

38 *On returning to the MRI machine:* Gary Small et al., "Your Brain on Google," *American Journal of Geriatric Psychiatry* 17, no. 2 (2009): 116–26.

38 *Your brain's ability to empathize:* Gary Small, interview with author, March 26, 2013.

38 *"the brighter the software":* Nicholas Carr, *The Shallows: What the Internet Is Doing to Our Brains* (New York: Norton, 2011), 216.

38 *The most startling example:* Kazuhisa Shibata et al., "Perceptual Learning Incepted by Decoded fMRI Neurofeedback Without Stimulus Presentation," *Science* 334, no. 6061 (December 9, 2011): 1413–15.

39 *"Think of a person watching a computer screen":* "Vision Scientists Demonstrate Innovative Learning Method," National Science Foundation, accessed January 10, 2014, http://www.nsf.gov/news/news_summ.jsp?cntn_id=122523&org=NSF&preview=false.

40 *Their boiled-down message:* "The Future of Higher Education," Pew Research Internet Project, accessed January 10, 2014, http://pewinternet.org/Reports/2012/Future-of-Higher-Education.aspx.

40 *Price promises that the young:* Ibid.

40 *"Some said they are already witnessing":* "Elon Studies the Future of 'Generation Always-On,'" Elon University, accessed January 10,

2014, http://www.elon.edu/e-net/Note.aspx?id=958393&board_ids=5%2C58&max=50.

41 *"design out of chaos"*: Daniel C. Dennett, *Darwin's Dangerous Idea: Evolution and the Meanings of Life* (New York: Simon & Schuster, 1995), 50.

45 *A 2013 study from the University of Michigan:* "The Generation X Report," University of Michigan Institute for Social Research, Winter 2013, accessed January 9, 2014, http://home.isr.umich.edu/files/2013/01/GenX_Vol2Iss2_print.pdf.

48 *"Other boys would not play with me"*: Anthony Trollope, *An Autobiography* (London: Penguin Classics, 1996), 32–33.

48 *"We must reserve a back shop"*: Michel de Montaigne, *The Complete Essays of Montaigne* (Stanford, Calif.: Stanford University Press, 1958), 177.

Chapter 3: Confession

49 *"The highest and most beautiful things"*: Søren Kierkegaard, *Either/Or* (Copenhagen: University Bookshop Reitzel, 1843), 89.

49 *The girl's name was Amanda Todd:* "Zeitgeist 2012," Google, accessed January 10, 2014, http://www.google.ca/zeitgeist/2012/#-the-world/people. (Whitney Houston and Kate Middleton held the two top spots that year.)

51 *She did not look into the camera:* "Amanda Todd's Mother Speaks Out," YouTube, accessed January 10, 2014, http://www.youtube.com/watch?v=-6dk9moSUqA.

52 *"it was something that needed to be watched by many"*: Carol Todd, e-mail message to author, January 13, 2014.

52 *seventeen million times:* Carol Todd, interview with author, April 19, 2013.

53 *Singapore children who were bullied online:* Thomas J. Holt, Grace Chee, and Esther Ng, "Exploring the Consequences of Bullying Victimization in a Sample of Singapore Youth," *International Criminal Justice Review* 23, no. 1 (2013): 5–24.

53 *22 percent of students:* Ibid.

55 *"every possible social and political problem"*: Evgeny Morozov, *The Net Delusion: The Dark Side of Internet Freedom* (New York: PublicAffairs, 2011), 312.

55 *"regardless of what you are looking at"*: Evgeny Morozov, *To Save Everything, Click Here: The Folly of Technological Solutionism* (New York: PublicAffairs, 2013), 357.

55 *"We bend to the inanimate"*: Sherry Turkle, *Alone Together: Why We Expect More from Technology and Less from Each Other* (New York: Basic Books, 2012), xii.

56 *"There are things, which you cannot tell your friends"*: Ibid., 51.

59 *"Extremely short exposures"*: Joseph Weizenbaum, *Computer Power and Human Reason: From Judgment to Calculation* (New York: W. H. Freeman & Co., 1976), 7.

59 *BMW was forced to recall*: Clifford Nass, "Sweet Talking Your Computer," *Wall Street Journal*, August 28, 2010, accessed January 12, 2014, http://online.wsj.com/news/articles/SB1000142405274870 3959704575453411132636080.

60 *"One day ladies will take their computers"*: Tom Siegfried, "A Mind from Math," *Science News*, vol. 181, issue 13 (2012): 26.

61 *According to Brian Christian's account*: Brian Christian, *The Most Human Human: What Artificial Intelligence Teaches Us About Being Alive* (New York: Anchor Books, 2012), 20.

62 *Infants at two or three months*: Maria Konnikova, "Infants Possess Intermingled Senses," *Scientific American*, accessed January 10, 2014, http://www.scientificamerican.com/article.cfm?id=infant-kandinskys.

63 *"This person thinks, 'I am damaged'"*: CNN has posted a transcript of that *Anderson Cooper 360°* segment here: http://transcripts.cnn .com/TRANSCRIPTS/1009/30/acd.01.html. A video of the segment can be found on YouTube: http://youtube.com/watch?v= bgxNItGmiC4.

66 *One Carnegie Mellon researcher*: Chloe Albanesius, "Social Security Numbers Revealed . . . with Facial-Recognition Software?," PCMag .com, August 1, 2011, accessed January 10, 2014, http://www .pcmag.com/article2/0,2817,2389540,00.asp.

68 *"the male gaze gone viral"*: Meghan Murphy, "Putting Selfies Under a Feminist Lens," *Georgia Straight*, accessed March 19, 2014, http:// www.straight.com/life/368086/putting-selfies-under-feminist-lens.

68 *"Self-tracking is . . . revelatory"*: Nora Young, *The Virtual Self: How Our Digital Lives Are Altering the World Around Us* (Toronto: McClelland & Stewart, 2012), 45.

69 *"Community feeling" had been a dominant theme*: Yalta T. Uhls and Patricia M. Greenfield, "The Rise of Fame: An Historical

Content Analysis," *Cyberpsychology: Journal of Psychosocial Research on Cyberspace* 5, no. 1 (2011): article 1, http://www .cyberpsychology.eu/view.php?cisloclanku=2011061601.

69 *British parents confirmed this position:* "Children Would Rather Become Popstars Than Teachers or Lawyers," *The Telegraph*, October 1, 2009, accessed January 10, 2014, http://www.telegraph .co.uk/education/educationnews/6250626/Children-would-rather -become-popstars-than-teachers-or-lawyers.html.

71 *"that which cannot be articulated":* Young, *Virtual Self,* 203.

Chapter 4: Public Opinion

73 *"We all do no end of feeling":* Mark Twain, *Tales, Speeches, Essays, and Sketches* (New York: Penguin Classics, 1994), 286–87.

73 *The world's arbiter of truth:* "Wikipedia: List of Hoaxes on Wikipedia," accessed January 13, 2014, http://en.wikipedia.org/ wiki/Wikipedia:List_of_hoaxes_on_Wikipedia.

73 *Four years later, I asked:* "Who is Erica Feldman . . . ?," snapshot from January 6, 2014, via Google's cache, http://webcache .googleusercontent.com/search?q=cache:Q77Wj1JfErsJ:wiki.answers .com/Q/Who_is_erica_feldman_the_one_that_invented_the_hair_ straightnener+&cd=1&hl=en&ct=clnk&gl=ca&client=firefox-a.

74 *There are even hoaxes about hoaxes:* "List of Fictitious People," Wikipedia.com, accessed January 15, 2014, http://en.wikipedia.org/ w/index.php?title=List_of_fictitious_people&diff=211003619& oldid=205705808.

74 *I see there are currently:* "Wikipedia:Statistics," Wikipedia, accessed January 17, 2014, http://en.wikipedia.org/wiki/ Wikipedia:Statistics.

75 *Printing Wikipedia in a book:* "Wikipedia:Size in Volumes," Wikipedia, accessed January 17, 2014, http://en.wikipedia.org/wiki/ Wikipedia:Size_in_volumes.

75 *"I guess we will just have to accept":* Roger C. Schank, *Making Minds Less Educated Than Our Own* (Taylor & Francis e-Library, 2008), vii.

78 *In 2013, only 12 cases:* Dave Craven, e-mail messages to author, June 26, 2013, and January 22, 2014.

79 *a stunning 91 percent of Wikipedia editors:* "Editor Survey 2011," Wikipedia: Meta-Wiki, accessed January 15, 2014, http://meta .wikimedia.org/wiki/Editor_Survey_2011.

79 *"the actual inventor" of the hair iron:* "Hoaxes, or Why Wikipedia Needs Flagged Revisions," accessed January 15, 2014, http://wikipediocracy.com/forum/viewtopic.php?t=647&p=12233.

79 *She died in New York:* "Madame C. J. Walker," MIT Inventor of the Week Archive, accessed January 15, 2014, http://web.mit.edu/invent/iow/cjwalker.html.

79 *Sadly, and perhaps inevitably:* Ibid.

80 *"Live the questions now":* Rainer Maria Rilke, *Letters to a Young Poet* (New York: Vintage, 1986), 34.

81 *"credentialed to uncredentialed":* David Weinberger, *Too Big to Know: Rethinking Knowledge Now That the Facts Aren't the Facts, Experts Are Everywhere, and the Smartest Person in the Room Is the Room* (New York: Basic Books, 2011), 67.

81 *"Let the wise instruct the wise":* Jonathan Rose, *The Intellectual Life of the British Working Classes* (New Haven, Conn., and London: Yale University Press, 2002), 223.

83 *"the duplication of the hermetic writings":* Elizabeth L. Eisenstein, *The Printing Revolution in Early Modern Europe,* 2nd ed. (New York: Cambridge University Press, 2005), 51.

83 *By the late 1800s:* Walter Benjamin, *The Work of Art in the Age of Mechanical Reproduction* (London: Penguin, 2008), 22–23.

84 *"the dominant mood of contemporary American culture":* William A. Henry, *In Defense of Elitism* (New York: Anchor Books, 1995), 177.

85 *"If market pricing is the only legitimate test":* Jaron Lanier, *Who Owns the Future?* (New York: Simon & Schuster, 2013), 360.

86 *"As more journals moved online":* Nicholas Carr, *The Shallows: What the Internet Is Doing to Our Brains* (New York: Norton, 2011), 217.

87 *the number hit 65.8 million:* "Yelp Reviewed," Statista, accessed January 16, 2014, http://socialtimes.com/files/2012/02/yelp-by-the-numbers-972.jpg.

87 *In 2013, Yelp enticed 117 million unique users per month:* "10 Things You Should Know About Yelp," Yelp: About Us, accessed January 17, 2014, http://www.yelp.ca/about.

87 *"Yelpers" have written 47 million reviews:* Ibid.

88 *A restaurateur in Ottawa's famous ByWard Market:* "Marisol Simoes Jailed: Co-owner of Kinki and Mambo in Ottawa Gets 90 Days for Defamation," *Huffington Post,* accessed January 16, 2014, http://www.huffingtonpost.ca/2012/11/16/marisol-simoes-jailed_n_2146205.html.

88   *"Today's internet is killing our culture"*: Andrew Keen, *The Cult of the Amateur* (New York: Doubleday/Currency, 2007).

91   *"the filter bubble"*: Eli Pariser, *The Filter Bubble: How the New Personalized Web Is Changing What We Read and How We Think* (New York: Penguin Press, 2011).

91   *Google announced that Google Maps:* Evegny Morozov, "My Map or Yours?," Slate, accessed September 4, 2013, http://www.slate .com/articles/technology/future_tense/2013/05/google_maps_ personalization_will_hurt_public_space_and_engagement.html.

92   *"Bullshit is unavoidable"*: Harry G. Frankfurt, *On Bullshit* (Princeton, N.J.: Princeton University Press, 2005), 63.

93   *"There I've gone and given away the plot"*: Dorothy Parker, "Far from Well," *The New Yorker*, October 20, 1928.

Chapter 5: Authenticity

94   *"But isn't everything here green?"*: L. Frank Baum, *The Wonderful Wizard of Oz* (New York: Knopf, 1992), 151–52.

95   *Over the next few years:* Author interview with Andrew Ng, July 11, 2013.

95   *Latest numbers show Coursera hosts:* "A Triple Milestone," Coursera Blog for October 23, 2013, accessed January 17, 2014, http://blog.coursera.org/post/64907189712/a-triple-milestone-107 -partners-532-courses-5-2.

97   *"We don't educate people as others wished"*: Max Chafkin, "Udacity's Sebastian Thrun, Godfather of Free Online Education, Changes Course," *Fast Company*, accessed December 2, 2013, http://www.fastcompany.com/3021473/udacity-sebastian-thrun -uphill-climb.

98   *"school was an invention of the printing press"*: Neil Postman, *Technopoly: The Surrender of Culture to Technology* (New York: Vintage, 1993), 10.

99   *Marshall McLuhan argues that whenever we amplify:* Marshall McLuhan, *Understanding Media: The Extensions of Man,* (Berkeley, Calif.: Ginkgo Press, 2003), 63–70.

100 *"Welcome to a world through glass"*: "What It Does—Google Glass," accessed September 5, 2013, http://www.google.com/glass/ start/what-it-does/.

100 *"the brightness and glory of the Emerald City"*: Baum, *Wonderful Wizard of Oz,* 88.

100 *"No more than in any other city"*: Ibid., 151–52.

100 *"a cathedral quits its site"*: Walter Benjamin, *The Work of Art in the Age of Mechanical Reproduction* (London: Penguin, 2008), 6.

101 *"The genuineness of a thing"*: Ibid., 7.

101 *"for the first time . . . a person is placed"*: Ibid., 19.

102 *A prime example is the Google Books project:* Robert Darnton, "The National Digital Public Library Is Launched!," *New York Review of Books,* accessed February 17, 2014. http://www.nybooks .com/articles/archives/2013/apr/25/national-digital-public-library -launched/.

103 *"precious old book"*: Stephan Füssel, *Gutenberg and the Impact of Printing* (Hampshire, UK: Ashgate Publishing, 2005), 198.

103 *His Bible's 1,282 pages:* John Man, *The Gutenberg Revolution: The Story of a Genius and an Invention That Changed the World* (New York: Random House, 2010), 146.

103 *The old "authentic" artifact:* Curt F. Bühler, *The Fifteenth-Century Book: The Scribes, the Printers, the Decorators* (Philadelphia: University of Pennsylvania Press, 1960), 16.

104 *our culture of electronic simulation:* Sherry Turkle, *Alone Together: Why We Expect More from Technology and Less from Each Other* (New York: Basic Books, 2012), 4.

105 *"because they're too busy"*: Geoffrey Miller, "Why We Haven't Met Any Aliens," *Seed,* accessed January 16, 2014, http://seedmagazine .com/content/article/why_we_havent_met_any_aliens/.

106 *"good enough for all practical purposes"*: E. M. Forster, "The Machine Stops," *Oxford and Cambridge Review* (November 1909).

106 *"At the end of the story"*: Jaron Lanier, *Who Owns the Future?* (New York: Simon & Schuster, 2013), 129.

107 *"Humanity has learned its lesson"*: Forster, "The Machine Stops."

107 *By one report, the aurorae lit up so brightly:* Sten F. Odenwald and James L. Green, "Bracing the Satellite Infrastructure for a Solar Superstorm," *Scientific American,* accessed January 16, 2014, http:// www.scientificamerican.com/article.cfm?id=bracing-for-a-solar -superstorm.

107 *Pete Riley, a scientist at Predictive Science:* Pete Riley, "On the Probability of Occurrence of Extreme Space Weather Events," *Space Weather* 10, no. 2 (2012), http://onlinelibrary.wiley.com/doi/10 .1029/2011SW000734/abstract.

107 *Great Britain's Royal Academy of Engineering:* "Extreme Space Weather," Royal Academy of Engineering, http://www.raeng.org .uk/news/publications/list/reports/space_weather_full_report _final.pdf.

107 *Such an event almost took place:* Pete Riley, e-mail message to author, June 25, 2013.

108 *"much of the modern industrialized and militarized world":* Joseph Weizenbaum, *Computer Power and Human Reason: From Judgment to Calculation* (New York: W. H. Freeman & Co., 1976).

108 *$2.6 trillion in damage:* "Solar Storm Risk to the North American Electric Grid," Lloyd's, accessed January 16, 2014, http://www.aer .com//sites/default/files/Solar_Storm_Risk_to_the_North_ American_Electric_Grid_0.pdf, and "Severe Space Weather Events: Understanding Societal and Economic Impacts," National Academies Press, http://www.nap.edu/catalog.php?record_id=12507.

Part 2 : Breaking Away

111 *"When from our better selves":* William Wordsworth, "The Prelude," in M. H. Abrams, gen. ed., *The Norton Anthology of English Literature*, vol. 2 (New York: Norton, 1993), 241.

Chapter 6: Attention!

113 *"In proportion as our inward life fails":* Brooks Atkinson, ed., *Walden and Other Writings of Henry David Thoreau* (New York: Modern Library, 1992), 723–24.

113 *"And none will hear the postman's knock":* W. H. Auden, "Night Mail," *The English Auden* (London and Boston: Faber & Faber, 1977).

114 *Animals, including humans, become obsessed:* Gary Small and Gigi Vorgan, *iBrain: Surviving the Technological Alteration of the Modern Mind* (New York: HarperCollins, 2008), 54–55.

115 *I'm not sure I'm as far gone:* Laura Vanderkam, "Stop Checking Your Email, Now," *Fortune*, October 8, 2012, http://management .fortune.cnn.com/2012/10/08/stop-checking-your-email-now/.

117 *"a minor fit of hysterics":* R. W. B. Lewis, *Edith Wharton: A Biography* (New York: Harper & Row, 1975).

118 *"fortify the wavering mind":* Seneca, *Dialogues and Essays* (New York: Oxford University Press, 2007), 139.

119 *"when it comes to the combination":* Tom Chatfield, *How to Thrive in the Digital Age* (London: Macmillan, 2012), 32.

121 *"whenever kids exceed the one to two hours":* "Media and Children," American Academy of Pediatrics, AAP Policy, http://www.aap.org/en-us/advocacy-and-policy/aap-health-initiatives/pages/media-and-children.aspx.

123 *Curiously, the largest hit:* "The Rise of E-Reading," Pew Research Center, April 5, 2012, http://libraries.pewinternet.org/files/legacy-pdf/The%20rise%20of%20e-reading%204.5.12.pdf.

123 *the National Endowment for the Arts (NEA) released a massive and scathing report:* "To Read or Not to Read: A Question of National Consequence," Research Report no. 47, November 2007, National Endowment for the Arts, http://arts.gov/sites/default/files/ToRead.pdf.

123 *"Anna Mikhailovna was already embracing her":* Leo Tolstoy, *War and Peace* (New York: Vintage Classics, 2008), 58.

126 *"At first she could not read":* Leo Tolstoy, *Anna Karenina* (New York: Knopf, 1992), 118.

126 *"Anna read and understood":* Ibid., 118.

130 *"The gaze-sensitive intervention":* Sidney D'Mello et al., "Gaze Tutor: A Gaze-Reactive Intelligent Tutoring System," *International Journal of Human-Computer Studies* 70, no. 5 (2012): 377–98.

132 *"To kill me?":* Tolstoy, *War and Peace,* 189.

132 *"not with his intellect, but with his whole being":* Ibid., 1060.

132 *"a causeless springtime feeling of joy":* Ibid., 423.

132 *"the so-called great men":* Ibid., 606.

133 *Milton sat down at his parents' home:* Thomas N. Corns, ed., *A Companion to Milton* (Oxford: Blackwell Publishing, 2003), 487.

134 *In the first draft of this letter:* David Masson, *Life of John Milton,* vol. 1 (London: Macmillan, 1859), 290–92.

134 *"None of this had even a hope":* "Steve Jobs' 2005 Stanford Commencement Address," YouTube, accessed March 21, 2014, http://www.youtube.com/watch?v=UF8uR6Z6KLc.

Chapter 7: Memory (The Good Error)

137 *"Forgetting used to be a failing":* James Gleick, *The Information: A History, a Theory, a Flood* (New York: Pantheon, 2011), 407.

139 *"That's surprising. I thought this was going to be difficult":* "Dr. Brenda Milner," CBC News, accessed January 16, 2014, http://www.cbc.ca/player/News/Health/ID/2323340807/.

141 *"The Internet allows us to know"*: John Brockman, ed., *Is the Internet Changing the Way You Think?: The Net's Impact on Our Minds and Future* (New York: Harper Perennial, 2011), 239.

141 *Perhaps we should side with philosopher Lewis Mumford*: Lewis Mumford, *The Myth of the Machine* (New York: Harcourt Brace Jovanovich, 1970), 182.

141 *Author Clive Thompson wondered*: Clive Thompson, "Your Outboard Brain Knows All," *Wired,* September 25, 2007, http://www.wired.com/techbiz/people/magazine/15-10/st_thompson.

142 *A team of psychologists has reported in* Science: Betsy Sparrow, Jenny Liu, and Daniel M. Wegner, "Google Effects on Memory," *Science* 333, no. 6043 (2011): 776–78.

144 *"Having thus made up his family"*: Seneca, *The Epistles of Lucius Annæus Seneca,* vol. 1 (London: W. Woodfall, 1786), 102–03.

145 *"Every dog-eared page"*: Brockman, *Is the Internet Changing the Way You Think?,* 300.

146 *"As the Web grew"*: Ibid., 300.

148 *"I consider that a man's brain"*: Sir Arthur Conan Doyle, *The Complete Sherlock Holmes,* vol. 1 (New York: Barnes & Noble Classics, 2003), 14.

154 *"are created in the present"*: Charles Fernyhough, "What Our Memories Tell Us About Ourselves," ideas.time.com, accessed March 21, 2014, http://ideas.time.com/2013/03/20/what-our-memories-tell-us-about-ourselves/.

154 *"Every time you recall a memory"*: "Scientists Explore the Illusion of Memory," CBC News, accessed January 16, 2014, http://www.cbc.ca/news/health/story/2013/01/03/health-inside-your-brain-memory-illusion.html.

154 *"Memory changes things"*: Achy Obejas, "My Interview with Jorge Luis Borges," accessed January 16, 2014, http://www.wbez.org/blog/achy-obejas/2011-08-24/my-interview-jorge-luis-borges-90978.

156 *In a 2013 paper*: Corina Sas and Steve Whittaker, "Design for Forgetting: Disposing of Digital Possessions After a Breakup," Proceedings of the SIGCHI Conference on Human Factors in Computing Systems, New York, 2013, http://people.ucsc.edu/~swhittak/papers/design_for_forgetting_chi_2013.pdf.

159 *In Manguel's* A History of Reading: Alberto Manguel, *A History of Reading* (Toronto: Vintage, 1998), 60–61.

160 *"The taste was that of the little piece of madeleine"*: Marcel Proust, *In Search of Lost Time,* vol. 1 (New York: Random House, 2003), 63–64.

Chapter 8: Hooking Up

167 *On a single Sunday:* "Grindr Sets Records," Grindr.com/blog, October 2, 2012.

167 *Meanwhile, Chatroulette links strangers:* Robert J. Moore, "Chatroulette Is 89 Percent Male, 47 Percent American, and 13 Percent Perverts," TechCrunch, accessed January 7, 2014, http://techcrunch.com/2010/03/16/chatroulette-stats-male-perverts/.

168 *Youths send homemade porn to one another:* "Snapchat's Expired Snaps Are Not Deleted, Just Hidden," *The Guardian,* accessed January 7, 2014, http://www.theguardian.com/media-network/partner-zone-infosecurity/snapchat-photos-not-deleted-hidden.

168 *Surveys conducted in 1980:* Eli J. Finkel et al., "Online Dating: A Critical Analysis from the Perspective of Psychological Science," *Psychological Science in the Public Interest* 13, no. 1 (2012): 3–66.

168 *Today, at least one in five:* "Online Dating Statistics," Statistic Brain, accessed January 16, 2014, http://www.statisticbrain.com/online-dating-statistics/.

168 *According to a massive 2010 BBC World Service report:* "New Global Poll Suggests Wide Enthusiasm for Online Dating," BBC World Service, accessed January 16, 2014, http://www.bbc.co.uk/pressoffice/pressreleases/stories/2010/02_february/13/poll.shtml.

168 *similar Pew Research Center work:* "Dating Digitally," Pew Internet & American Life Project, accessed March 21, 2014, http://www.pewinternet.org/2013/10/21/online-dating-relationships/.

169 *83 percent of us:* I-Mei Lin and Erik Peper, "Psychophysiological Patterns During Cell Phone Text Messaging: A Preliminary Study," *Applied Psychophysiology and Biofeedback* 34, no. 1 (2009): 53–57.

169 *"as long as a guy can keep clicking":* Gary Wilson, "The Great Porn Experiment," TEDxGlasgow, accessed March 24, 2014, http://www.youtube.com/watch?v=wSF82AwSDiU.

172 *According to Trussler's report:* "Pride, Prejudice, & Determinants of Health," Community-Based Research Centre, 2012, accessed January 16, 2014, http://cbrc.net/sites/default/files/PPDYouthF%20-AC.pdf.

173 *When 606 students were canvassed:* Donald S. Strassberg et al., "Sexting by High School Students: An Exploratory and Descriptive Study," *Archives of Sexual Behavior* 42, no. 1 (2013): 15–21.

173 *On Grindr, too, it is the digital natives:* "Happy Birthday Grindr!," Grindr Blog for March 25, 2013, http://grindr.com/blog/2013/03.

174 *Comparison of the two shows:* Michelle Rotermann, "Trends in Teen Sexual Behaviour and Condom Use," Statistics Canada, *Health Reports* 19, no. 3 (September 2008), http://www.statcan.gc.ca/pub/82-003-x/2008003/article/10664-eng.pdf.

174 *In fact, the only significant change:* Michelle Rotermann, "Sexual Behaviour and Condom Use of 15- to 24-Year-Olds in 2003 and 2009/2010," Statistics Canada, *Health Reports* 23, no. 1 (March 2012), accessed January 16, 2014, http://www.statcan.gc.ca/pub/82-003-x/2012001/article/11632-eng.htm.

176 *"The knight departing for new adventures":* Simone de Beauvoir, *The Second Sex* (New York: Knopf, 1953), 658.

177 *Mobile users check their PlentyofFish:* Markus Frind, interview with author, July 31, 2013.

179 *Marshall McLuhan, in* The Gutenberg Galaxy, *writes about the garden of senses:* Marshall McLuhan, *The Gutenberg Galaxy* (Toronto: University of Toronto Press, 1962), 21.

183 *PlentyofFish is especially solicitous:* Markus Frind, interview with author, July 31, 2013.

Chapter 9: How to Absent Oneself

184 *Ah, where have they gone":* Milan Kundera, *Slowness*, trans. Linda Asher (New York: HarperCollins, 1996), 3.

188 *"intrude itself":* Joseph Weizenbaum, *Computer Power and Human Reason: From Judgment to Calculation* (London: Penguin, 1984), 18.

188 *"psychic distance . . . never natural":* Postman, *Technopoly*, 185.

189 *"one good test of whether an economy is humanistic":* Lanier, *Who Owns the Future?*, 365.

192 *"You have to see that there is more":* William Powers, *Hamlet's BlackBerry: A Practical Philosophy for Building a Good Life in the Digital Age* (New York: Harper Perennial, 2011), 165.

198 *"The surface of the earth is soft"*: Henry David Thoreau, *Walden* (New York: Everyman's Library, 1992), 286.

198 *"I did not wish to live what was not life"*: Ibid., 80.

199 *"I did not wish to take a cabin passage"*: Ibid., 286.

200 *"The whistle of the locomotive"*: Ibid., 103.

200 *"And it is worth the while to be warned"*: Ibid., 105.

201 *"They wanted to make inquiries about themselves"*: Glenn Gould, speaking in the documentary film *Genius Within: The Inner Life of Glenn Gould* (2009), directed by Michèle Hozer and Peter Raymont.

202 *We know that the spread of writing:* Harold A. Innis, *The Bias of Communication* (Toronto: University of Toronto Press, 2008), 8.

202 *We know that "the immortal inconclusiveness of Plato"*: Ibid., 10.

202 *"through a veil of print"*: Elizabeth L. Eisenstein, *The Printing Press as an Agent of Change* (Cambridge, UK: Cambridge University Press, 1982), 6.

203 *"by far the greater number of new ideas"*: Anthony Storr, *Solitude: A Return to the Self* (New York: Free Press, 2005), 198.

203 *"men's greatest achievements are the products of their seclusion"*: Seneca, *Dialogues and Essays* (New York: Oxford University Press, 2007), 119.

204 *"It is, however, necessary to combine the two things"*: Ibid., 137.

204 *The historian of ideas Noga Arikha:* John Brockman, ed., *Is the Internet Changing the Way You Think?: The Net's Impact on Our Minds and Future* (New York: Harper Perennial, 2011), 42.

205 *"I waver"*: Ibid., 42.

205 *"Those who experience the first onset"*: McLuhan, *Gutenberg Galaxy,* 27.

Epilogue: What Comes Across, What Stays Behind

208 *"the historical Luddites were neither childish nor naïve"*: Neil Postman, *Technopoly: The Surrender of Culture to Technology* (New York: Vintage, 1993), 43.

INDEX